CORRECTIONAL SUPERVISION

CORRESPONDENCE COURSE

LEGAL ISSUES

BOOK III

a publication of the
AMERICAN CORRECTIONAL ASSOCIATION
4380 Forbes Boulevard
Lanham, MD 20706-4322
(301) 918-1800

ACA STAFF

John J. Greene, III
Director
Training and Contracts

Diane E. Geiman
Project Director
Correspondence Courses

Patricia E. Cece
Assistant Writer/Editor

Denise K. Flannery
Assistant Editor

EXECUTIVE COMMITTEE

PRESIDENT
Perry M. Johnson

PRESIDENT-ELECT
Bobbie L. Huskey

IMMEDIATE PAST-PRESIDENT
Helen G. Corrothers

VICE PRESIDENT
Dennis S. Avery

TREASURER
M. Tamara Holden

BOARD OF GOVERNORS
REPRESENTATIVE
Betty K. Adams

BOARD OF GOVERNORS
REPRESENTATIVE
Gail D. Hughes

EXECUTIVE DIRECTOR
James A. Gondles, Jr.

The American Correctional Association reserves the right to reproduce, publish, translate, or otherwise use, and to authorize others to publish and use all or any part of the copyrighted material contained in this publication.

ISBN 0-929310-95-0
Copyright 1993 by the American Correctional Association

Acknowledgments

The revised *Correctional Supervision Correspondence Course* was developed by Capitol Communication Systems, Incorporated (#7 Chelsea House, 2411 Crofton Lane, Crofton, Maryland 21114). Capitol Communication System's staff includes:

Project Manager	Thomas A. Sutty
Writer/Editor	Carla M. Heath
Graphic Designer	Margaret J. Grabowski
Typesetters	Judi M. Morgan Michelle L. Duvall
Photographer	David S. Sutty

ACA REVIEW COMMITTEE

Special thanks to our reviewers who guided us during the development process.

> William C. Collins
> Attorney At Law
> Olympia, WA
>
> Lt. Gary F. Cornelius
> Fairfax County Sheriff's Office
> Fairfax, Virginia

Foreword

The American Correctional Association is pleased to offer the revised *Correctional Supervision Correspondence Course*. The original course published in 1984 has been used throughout the corrections profession as the basis for supervisory training. We designed the new version to teach the correctional staff of today how to become the supervisory leaders of tomorrow.

Correctional supervisors are the most important link in the correctional management team. These leaders are responsible not only for maintaining good morale but also for ensuring smooth operations. Every institution, facility or agency relies on its supervisors to provide leadership which may inspire the staff to achieve an even higher level of performance.

All the subject matter in *Correctional Supervision* will provide you with practical training that is directly related to the roles and duties of the correctional supervisor. Most of the chapters have been extensively revised, including Interpersonal Communication, Parts I and II; Conducting Performance Appraisals; Civil Liability; and The Disciplinary Process. In addition, new chapters have been created, such as Roles of the Correctional Supervisor, and Standards of Ethical Conduct. Moreover, a case study was written to help readers test their comprehension of the principles taught throughout the course.

The self-instructional format of this course offers you many advantages. You may study during your free time and work at your own pace. Also, by completing this course, and others like it, you may increase your chances for promotion.

We hope that *Correctional Supervision* enriches your life, both professionally and personally. Best wishes in your endeavors within the corrections profession.

Sincerely,
James A. Gondles, Jr.
Executive Director

Course Outline

The *Correctional Supervision Correspondence Course* consists of four books:

BOOK ONE—SUPERVISION IN THE 90'S

    Chapter 1: Introduction to Supervision
    Chapter 2: Roles of the Correctional Supervisor
    Chapter 3: Standards of Ethical Conduct
    Chapter 4: Stress Management Techniques

BOOK TWO—WORKING WITH STAFF

    Chapter 1: Interpersonal Communication, Part One
    Chapter 2: Interpersonal Communication, Part Two
    Chapter 3: Conducting Performance Appraisals
    Chapter 4: Saving Time and Energy

BOOK THREE—LEGAL ISSUES

    Chapter 1: Discrimination in the Workplace
    Chapter 2: Civil Liability in Corrections
    Chapter 3: The Disciplinary Process

BOOK FOUR—CASE STUDY

Table of Contents

BOOK THREE — LEGAL ISSUES

    Chapter 1: Discrimination in the Workplace III–1

                  Answer Key III–54

    Chapter 2: Civil Liability in Corrections III–65

                  Answer Key III–125

    Chapter 3: The Disciplinary Process III–135

                  Answer Key III–176

    References III–183

CHAPTER 1

Discrimination in the Workplace

Objectives

At the end of this chapter, you will be able to:

▶ List at least four recent social forces that have caused employees to be more sensitive to the rights of individual workers.

▶ Define Equal Employment Opportunity (EEO) laws.

▶ List the areas of employment that are effected by EEO laws.

▶ List at least four laws passed to protect citizens from discrimination.

▶ Explain the difference between discrimination and harassment.

▶ List one of the three conditions that must be present for sexual harassment to exist.

▶ List the four acts that form the range of sexual harassment.

▶ List a supervisor's responsibilities in maintaining a work environment free from harassment.

Introduction

As you have learned, the goal of good supervision is for all employees to perform at their highest level. Employees tend to perform well and grow in a positive climate—a place with good morale, fair policies and procedures, and competent supervision. The effective supervisor helps build this positive climate by communicating clearly and treating all employees as equals.

Equal treatment means that a supervisor doesn't play favorites or treat certain individuals differently than the rest of the group. In other words, the effective supervisor does not discriminate against any employee.

Discrimination is treating a person or group of people differently because of their race, color, religion, sex or national origin. The person is not only treated differently, but also as an inferior. Therefore, he or she is excluded from opportunities.

Unfortunately, in our country, the most common victims of discrimination have been and continue to be minorities. Sociologist Joseph Gittler defines minorities as "those groups whose members occupy a relatively low status within the social structure due to a lack of perceived power." Or simply put, minorities are those who have very little economic, political or social power within the broader society.

During the past few decades, many of these groups became more aware of the extent of the discrimination against them. Consequently, they mounted strong campaigns to right the injustice. Their efforts led to the passage of local, state and federal laws to protect the rights of many minorities.

This chapter will cover some of the federal legislation designed to prohibit discrimination. The primary focus will be on sexual harassment, and your role as a supervisor in recognizing and preventing it.

Changes in the Workplace

Many social forces have changed the way we do business in the workplace and have made all employers, including governments, more sensitive to the rights of individual workers. These powerful forces include:

- The Civil Rights Movement
- The Women's Movement
- An increasing number of women in the workforce
- An increasing number of females as heads of households, needing a full-time job
- A concern for the mentally and physically disabled
- An increasingly culturally diverse workforce
- More unionization among government workers

All levels of government, particularly the federal level, responded to these forces by passing several laws to protect the rights of those groups that traditionally have suffered discrimination. More properly stated, this legislation was passed to protect the rights of *all* citizens.

List three social forces that have changed the workplace.

- _____
- _____
- _____

(7)

EEO Laws

The legislative measures designed to protect the rights of citizens in the workplace are called Equal Employment Opportunity (EEO) laws. As the name implies, the intent of these laws is to assure equal treatment of all workers. This means that workers who belong to minority groups have the same rights as workers who belong to "majority" groups.

These laws affect all areas of employment, including:

▶ Recruitment

▶ Selection

▶ Compensation

▶ Discipline

▶ Treatment

The EEO laws are intended to

_____

_____.

(10)

List three areas of employment affected by EEO laws.

• _____

• _____

• _____

(14)

CHAPTER 1: DISCRIMINATION IN THE WORKPLACE III—5

Implications for Supervisors

The basic principle of the EEO laws is that employees should be treated as individuals, not as members of a group. In other words, you have *people* working for you—Joe and John and Jane—not a "black," an "Indian," and a "woman." Decisions about hiring, promoting, training, disciplining or any other work-related matter must be made on how that person is performing the job.

Let's look at an example. You are supervising a unit that has two white male officers, three white female officers, and one black male officer. You must decide which officer goes to a training class to learn basic supervisory techniques. This class is the first step toward a promotion to supervisor. How do you decide which officer to send?

You ask yourself questions such as:

▶ Which officer has shown interest in supervision?

▶ Which officer gets along well with the other officers?

▶ Which officer has a thorough knowledge of institution procedures?

▶ Which officer has the most experience on the job?

You evaluate each officer's merits—his or her performance, work habits, job skills. You DO NOT make your decision on the basis of gender or race.

Respecting the civil rights of your staff will go a long way toward creating a positive climate in the workplace.

TRUE/FALSE EEO laws prohibit treating people as members of a group.

(18)

TRUE/FALSE You should make decisions about work-related matters based on whether or not you like the person involved.

(22)

Federal Legislation Overview

The concept of protecting individual rights has been around since the birth of our country. Our forefathers created the Bill of Rights (in the Constitution) for this purpose. Later, after the Civil War, Congress passed legislation that offered further protection.

While civil rights amendments/laws have been in existence for over 100 years, many of them were not actively enforced until the twentieth century. In fact, Congress didn't create federal agencies with power to enforce civil rights laws until the 1960's.

Considerable progress has been made, however, in the past few decades. And today, we have even more protection under recent federal legislation.

Constitutional amendments and laws passed to protect citizens from discrimination include:

- Fifth Amendment, U.S. Constitution, 1791
- Fourteenth Amendment, U.S. Constitution, 1868
- Civil Rights Act of 1964, amended by EEO Act of 1972
- The Age Discrimination Act of 1967
- The Rehabilitation Act of 1973
- The Americans with Disabilities Act of 1990
- The Civil Rights Act of 1991
- The Family and Medical Leave Act of 1993

We will review each of these briefly, then concentrate on the issue of sexual harassment.

List at least five laws passed to protect citizens from discrimination.

- _____
- _____
- _____
- _____
- _____

(1)

The _____

was the first legislation to protect citizens' rights in the United States.

(33)

CHAPTER 1: DISCRIMINATION IN THE WORKPLACE

Federal Legislation
Overview (continued)

FIFTH AMENDMENT, U.S. CONSTITUTION—1791

To put a historical perspective on discrimination, we can go all the way back to 1791 when the Fifth Amendment was adopted as part of the Bill of Rights. The Fifth Amendment states that *no person shall be deprived of life, liberty or property without due process.*

This means that the government can't take action against someone without giving her the opportunity to defend herself. Due process is the set of principles that must be followed to ensure a fair proceeding.

The Fifth Amendment refers to actions of the federal government, including when the government is the employer. As a correctional worker, you are probably employed by a government—either local, state or federal. If you work for a correctional facility run by the federal government, the Fifth Amendment protects you against discrimination.

The Fifth Amendment covers actions by the federal government, including the government as the

_____.

(5)

TRUE/FALSE The interest of the federal government in prohibiting discrimination started in 1960.

(38)

The Fifth Amendment states that no person shall be deprived of _____ , _____

or _____ **without due process.**

(9)

Federal Legislation
Overview (continued)

FOURTEENTH AMENDMENT, U.S. CONSTITUTION—1868

This amendment states that *no **State** shall deprive any person of life, liberty or property without due process of law, nor deny to any person within its jurisdiction the equal protection of the law.*

The Fourteenth Amendment applies to correctional staff who work in state and local facilities or agencies. If you are a state or local employee, you are protected from arbitrary or discriminatory employment actions. And, you are entitled to due process.

The Fifth and Fourteenth Amendments are used less often in lawsuits than the more recent civil rights laws we'll cover later.

TRUE/FALSE   The Fourteenth Amendment and the Fifth Amendment are identical.
(13)

TRUE/FALSE   Both the Fifth and the Fourteenth Amendments are used often in lawsuits.
(17)

The Fifth Amendment covers the employment rights of _____ workers, while the Fourteenth Amendment protects the rights of _____ employees.
(24)

CHAPTER 1: DISCRIMINATION IN THE WORKPLACE   III—9

Federal Legislation Overview (continued)

CIVIL RIGHTS ACT OF 1964—Title VII Amended by the EEO Act of 1972

The Civil Rights Act of 1964 is the law upon which most anti-discrimination cases are based. This law was amended in 1972, and again in 1991, to provide further clarification and additional remedies in cases of employment discrimination. Its purpose is to deter harassment and discrimination in the workplace.

In fact, the Act prohibits membership or employment discrimination on the basis of race, color, religion, sex or national origin. And, it also specifies the remedies that are available to persons who were discriminated against.

The law applies to private employers with 15 or more employees, all state and local government employers, unions and employment agencies. Most correctional staff, therefore, are covered by the Civil Rights Act.

THE AGE DISCRIMINATION ACT—1967

The Age Discrimination Act of 1967 *prohibits discrimination against employees between ages 40 and 70 because of their age.* While the law applies mainly to state and local governments, a special provision covers federal employees.

The Civil Rights Act applies to:

- _____
- _____
- _____
- _____

(28)

The Civil Rights Act prohibits employment discrimination based on _____ , _____ , _____ , _____ **or national origin.**

(35)

The Age Discrimination Act applies to persons between the ages of _____ **and** _____ .

(40)

Federal Legislation
Overview (continued)

THE REHABILITATION ACT—1973

The Rehabilitation Act of 1973 prohibits discrimination against people with physical or mental handicaps, or perceived handicaps, which substantially limit employment. This law applies only to agencies receiving federal funds which, of course, includes most correctional agencies.

THE AMERICANS WITH DISABILITIES ACT—1990

The Americans with Disabilities Act (ADA) prohibits discrimination against persons with physical and mental disabilities in two areas: employment and "access."

The ADA protects disabled persons before and after they are hired. People who are qualified for a job cannot be denied an opportunity to compete for it simply because of their disability. Moreover, organizations are required to "reasonably accommodate" the disabilities of a job applicant or employee.

There are few physically or mentally handicapped employees in corrections, however. The reason lies in the following exception to the ADA: If an organization can show that hiring the disabled for a particular job would pose a *"direct threat to the health or safety of the persons or others,"* it is exempt from hiring them.

The ADA affects the areas of _____
and _____ .

(2)

Federal Legislation
Overview (continued)

The right to access is the area that most concerns jails and prisons. The term "access" refers to the ability of disabled persons to enjoy the "benefits of the services, programs or activities of a public entity." Generally, this means that both inmates and visitors who are disabled must be able to go to the same places and do the same things as everyone else.

For example, an inmate's mother, who uses a wheelchair, cannot be denied visitation privileges simply because there is no ramp up to the door of the visiting room. The facility must make any construction changes that are necessary to allow her access. The same is true of a physically disabled inmate.

Similarly, an inmate with a physical or mental disability has the right to take part in programs. Thus, a facility must make "reasonable accommodations" for these disabled inmates. What is "reasonable" will depend on the particular situation. In some cases, something comparable might be offered to the inmate.

The ADA will not cause big changes in your day-to-day supervision. But you need to be aware of and respect the rights of disabled inmates. And, you need to make sure that your subordinates do the same. For instance, suppose a disabled inmate asks to attend a class that is held in a location which is physically impossible to reach. You and your staff should make all reasonable arrangements so that the inmate can attend the class. The reasonable arrangements should be covered in your policies and procedures. If not, consult your superior before you take any action.

The ADA prohibits discrimination against _____

_____.

(6)

Federal Legislation
Overview (continued)

THE CIVIL RIGHTS ACT—1991
(Title 3—"The Glass Ceiling Act")

In 1991, Congress found that minorities were still under-represented in management and decision-making positions in many organizations. Congress also discovered that artificial barriers existed to the advancement of women and minorities in the workplace. A law was passed, therefore, to increase public awareness of this bias.

The law does not specify any penalties or remedies for discrimination against women and minorities. But it provides an award for employers "whose practices and policies promote opportunities for, and eliminate artificial barriers to, the advancement of women and minorities." In addition, it has created a commission to study promotional practices.

The actual impact of this law on corrections is as yet unknown. However, you *can* make sure that the result is a positive one in your unit. Be sure to treat your staff as individuals, and reward good performance without consideration of sex, race or age.

The "Glass Ceiling Act" awards employees "whose practices and policies promote opportunities and eliminate barriers to the advancement of women and minorities."

The goal of the "Glass Ceiling Act" is to increase the number of women and minorities in _____ _____ positions.
(3)

CHAPTER 1: DISCRIMINATION IN THE WORKPLACE

Federal Legislation
Overview (continued)

THE FAMILY AND MEDICAL LEAVE ACT—1993

The Family and Medical Leave Act, signed into law on February 5, 1993, applies to organizations that have more than 50 employees. This act enables employees to take leave for medical reasons, for the birth or adoption of a child, or for the care of a child, spouse or parent who has a serious health condition. The law states that employees may take up to 12 weeks of unpaid leave from their jobs in a one year period—for a family or medical emergency. So, once a worker's normal leave is used up, he or she may take additional time off, without pay, up to a total of 12 weeks.

To be eligible for emergency leave, the employee must have worked for the same employer for at least 1,250 hours over the last 12 months. The employee must make a reasonable effort not to unduly disrupt the operations of the agency, and must provide notice of the intention to take leave, if possible. For example, John Harley would like to stay home for three weeks to help his wife after the birth of their third child. He only has one week of vacation remaining.

Harley must notify his supervisor at least one month in advance of his intention to take three weeks off—one week of vacation, and two weeks of unpaid leave.

In the case of a medical emergency, obviously, such advance notification is not possible. The employee must, however, provide certification from a health care provider that states the starting date and probable duration of the illness.

As a supervisor, you may be affected by this law if one of your staff takes leave to handle a medical or family crisis. You must allow your subordinate to take the leave, and you may not take any disciplinary action as a result of the extra time used. Also, leave used under this act must not cause a negative mark on the performance appraisal. It will probably be inconvenient, but you will have to rearrange your remaining staff, and continue all your unit's activities as usual.

The Family and Medical Leave Act allows an employee to take up to _____ of unpaid leave for a family or medical emergency.

(12)

TRUE/FALSE You can start disciplinary procedures against a subordinate who is off work for six weeks while his wife is in the hospital.

(23)

III–14   CHAPTER 1: DISCRIMINATION IN THE WORKPLACE

Summary of EEO Legislation

FIFTH AMENDMENT, U.S. CONSTITUTION—1791

- "No person shall be deprived of life, liberty or property without due process"
- Applies to the federal government as an employer
- Requires due process

FOURTEENTH AMENDMENT, U.S. CONSTITUTION—1868

- "No state shall deprive any person of life, liberty or property without due process, nor deny any person the equal protection of the law"
- Applies to state and local governments as employers
- Forbids arbitrary or discriminatory employment actions
- Requires due process

CIVIL RIGHTS ACT OF 1964—TITLE VII, As Amended by EEO Act of 1972

- "Prohibits membership or employment discrimination on the basis of race, color, religion, sex or national origin"
- Applies to private employers with 15 or more employees
- Applies to state and local governments as employers
- Applies to unions and employment agencies

AGE DISCRIMINATION ACT—1967

- "Prohibits discrimination against employees between ages 40 and 70"
- Applies to state and local governments as employers
- A special provision of the law covers federal employees

Summary of EEO Legislation (continued)

REHABILITATION ACT—1973

▶ "Prohibits discrimination against persons with physical or mental handicaps which limit employment"

▶ Applies only to agencies which receive federal funds

AMERICANS WITH DISABILITIES ACT—1990

▶ "Prohibits discrimination against persons with physical or mental handicaps"

▶ Applies to all employers

▶ All "public entities"—offices and businesses—must provide easy access to persons with physical or mental handicaps

THE CIVIL RIGHTS ACT of 1991 (Title 3—"The Glass Ceiling Act")

▶ Encourages the promotion of women and minorities to decision-making positions

▶ Gives national awards for employers whose practices and policies promote women and minorities

FAMILY AND MEDICAL LEAVE ACT—1993

▶ Entitles employees to take up to 12 weeks of unpaid leave in a one-year period for medical or family emergencies

▶ Applies to all employers with more than 50 employees

▶ Employee must have worked for the same employer for at least 1,250 hours over the last 12 months prior to taking extra leave

▶ No personnel or disciplinary action can be taken against an employee who takes emergency leave

EEO Legislation Review

Match the following legislation to its measure/effect/requirement.

1. Fifth Amendment, 1791
2. Fourteenth Amendment, 1868
3. Civil Rights Act, 1964
4. Age Discrimination Act, 1967
5. Americans with Disabilities Act, 1990
6. Civil Rights Act, 1991
7. Family and Medical Leave Act, 1993

_____ A. Prohibits discrimination against 60-year-old workers

_____ B. Encourages moving women into management positions

_____ C. Prohibits employment based on religion

_____ D. States that no state shall deprive any person of life, liberty or property without due process, nor deny equal protection of the law

_____ E. Allows extra, unpaid leave for emergencies

_____ F. Prohibits membership discrimination based on race

_____ G. Prohibits discrimination against individuals with physical and mental handicaps

(71)

Sexual Harassment—Background

Sexual harassment in the workplace is rapidly emerging as one of the most significant and controversial labor relations issues of the 1990's.

The topic was the subject of several Congressional hearings that received extensive media coverage in 1979 and 1980. In 1991, the Senate hearings concerning the nomination of Clarence Thomas to the Supreme Court raised the issue again. Subsequent reports on TV and in the print media made sexual harassment a primary topic of discussion. Public awareness of the issue is now greater than ever before.

In 1980, the Merit System Protection Board (MSPB) surveyed 23,000 federal employees. The survey found that 40% of the women and 15% of the men had experienced sexual harassment in the 24 months prior to the survey. In 1992, the Equal Employment Opportunity Commission reported that 7,496 lawsuits concerning sexual harassment were filed, 9% of which were filed by men.

Not only is sexual harassment a violation of individual rights, it also results in a huge loss of time and money. The benefits awarded in sexual harassment cases totaled over $6 million in 1992, twice the amount awarded in 1991. But the real cost is in the legal fees, decreased productivity and the lowering of employee morale. Once a sexual harassment charge has been brought, it takes time for people to put it behind them and move on after the situation is resolved.

TRUE/FALSE   Sexual harassment at work is one of the most significant and controversial labor relations issues of the 1990s.
(25)

TRUE/FALSE   Only women experience sexual harassment.
(30)

Sexual Harassment—
Background (continued)

As you recall, the Civil Rights Act of 1964, as amended, prohibited employment or membership discrimination on the basis of race, color, religion, sex or national origin. In 1980, *sexual harassment* was defined as part of *sex discrimination,* and guidelines defining it and prohibiting it in the workplace were published by various federal agencies, including the Equal Employment Opportunity Commission (EEOC).

The primary authority for prohibiting sex discrimination, and therefore sexual harassment, is Title VII of the Civil Rights Act. It is the major legislation cited in discrimination suits, and is one of the major concerns of the EEOC at the present time. *Both sex discrimination and harassment are prohibited by Title VII and are against the law.*

DIFFERENCES BETWEEN DISCRIMINATION AND HARASSMENT

Many people have difficulty understanding the difference between sex discrimination and sexual harassment. It may help to remember that *discrimination* is a general term, while *harassment* is a specific term. The following pages will explain the relationship between sexual harassment and discrimination.

Both sex discrimination and harassment are prohibited by Title VII and are against the law.

Title VII of the Civil Rights Act prohibits _____,
and therefore sexual _____.
(20)

TRUE/FALSE   The EEOC defined sexual harassment as a part of sex discrimination.
(16)

CHAPTER 1: DISCRIMINATION IN THE WORKPLACE

Sex Discrimination

Discrimination is a broad term and is usually defined as "differential treatment." This means that one person is treated differently than another person.

Some examples of discrimination are:

▶ Passing over an individual for promotion because he or she is near retirement. (Age discrimination)

▶ Requiring females to answer questions not asked of males during an employment interview. (Gender discrimination)

▶ Prohibiting female correctional officers from working the night shift in a male unit. (Sex discrimination)

In the workplace, showing *favoritism toward* or *bias against* an employee because of his or her gender is sex discrimination, and it is against the law.

The victims of sex discrimination may be either male or female, and their harassers may be their supervisors or co-workers.

Victims of sex discrimination may be male or female.

Discrimination is defined as "_____.''
(43)

Showing favoritism toward or bias against an employee because of his or her gender is called _____.
(48)

Sex Discrimination (continued)

It wasn't long ago that female correctional officers worked only in female institutions. There were a few women working in the administrative offices of correctional facilities, but the cellblocks were totally staffed by men. For this reason, some correctional officers you supervise may be uncomfortable with women as co-workers. These men may feel threatened by this "invasion" of the all-male workplace. They may think that they will lose their jobs to women because of EEOC guidelines, and they may generally be hostile to their female co-workers.

As a supervisor (and probably a former line officer), you may also feel uncomfortable with the female members of your staff. You may unconsciously judge their performance by a different, higher standard than you apply to the male officers. You may give them "easier" assignments without realizing that you are discriminating against them.

Once you are aware of these potential problems, you will be able to prevent, and stop, sex discrimination.

Check the statements that are true.

_____ A. Harassers may be both supervisors and co-workers.

_____ B. Sexual harassment is part of sex discrimination.

_____ C. The Civil Rights Act of 1964 prohibited discrimination based on merit.

_____ D. Although sex discrimination is against the law, sexual harassment is not.

_____ E. The Civil Rights Act of 1964 is the major legislation cited in discrimination suits.

_____ F. Sexual harassment not only violates individual rights but it also represents a huge dollar drain due to lost productivity and legal fees.

(36)

Sexual Harassment

While sex discrimination is broadly defined and covers a variety of actions, sexual harassment has a much narrower meaning. It is a specific form of sex discrimination.

In 1980, the EEOC issued formal guidelines defining sexual harassment and describing conditions under which it can legally be found to exist. Simply put, the EEOC guidelines define sexual harassment as *uninvited conduct with sexual overtones in the workplace.*

Some examples are:

▶ A supervisor who promises to promote someone if the candidate will date her is blatantly practicing sexual harassment because the conduct has explicit sexual overtones.

▶ A supervisor who hints that a female correctional officer can improve her performance rating by meeting with him after work is practicing sexual harassment.

▶ Employees who continually pat or pinch employees of the opposite sex, or who make comments about the others' appearance are guilty of sexual harassment.

Sexual harassment is uninvited conduct with sexual overtones in the workplace.

Sexual Harassment Review

Check the examples of discrimination.

_____ A. Not hiring a 40-year-old man who is qualified

_____ B. Not hiring a woman even though she is unqualified

_____ C. Asking women questions not asked of men during an employment interview

_____ D. Not promoting a person who is near retirement age

(4)

Sexual harassment is a specific form of _____.

(8)

The EEOC defined sexual harassment as "uninvited conduct with _____ in the workplace."

(11)

TRUE/FALSE   You should ask a female employee about her future plans to have children before you approve her promotion.

(15)

TRUE/FALSE   A male supervisor asking a female officer for a date is an example of sexual harassment.

(19)

Sexual Harassment— Behavior and Conditions

Let's look at the EEOC guidelines more closely to see exactly what kind of *behavior* is prohibited and the *conditions* that must be present for sexual harassment to exist.

BEHAVIOR

The EEOC guidelines say that sexual harassment is unwelcome or uninvited conduct with sexual overtones in the workplace. The key words are "unwelcome or uninvited." The EEOC is *not* trying to legislate the normal course of male-female attraction and relations. It is trying to protect men and women from comments and actions that are demeaning and abusive. Unwelcome and uninvited conduct can be either physical or verbal.

Physical conduct can range from the seemingly accidental bump to a blatant grab. Some examples are:

- Officer Jose bumps into the back of Officer Maria as they take the count.
- Officer Joan frequently pats Officer Warren on the knee as they work in the Control Room.
- Supervisor Lewis grabs Officer Mary and tries to kiss her when they're alone in his office.

Unwelcome or uninvited conduct can also be verbal, such as off-color or risqué jokes, comments about the body, sexual remarks, catcalls, whistles, or sexual invitations. Some examples are:

- Officer Darryl whistles at Inmate Marge every time he walks by her.
- Supervisor Tanya whispers "nice buns" to Officer George.
- Supervisor Vince tells Officer Gina, "If you want this promotion, let's talk about it at my place tonight."

Keep in mind that there will be normal male-female attraction in the workplace. If both parties welcome this attraction and any subsequent interaction, then it is not sexual harassment. For example, if Officer John asks co-worker Jane, "How about a drink after work?" and she replies, "I thought you'd never ask," that conduct is not unwelcome. It may be inappropriate on the job, but it is not illegal.

Sexual Harassment—
Behavior and Conditions (continued)

Here are a few rough guidelines for determining if behavior is appropriate for the workplace:

▶ Would you do it or say it in front of your spouse or your parents?

▶ Would you do it or say it in front of a co-worker of the same sex?

▶ How would you feel if your mother or father were subjected to the same words or behavior?

▶ How would you feel if another person of the same sex said or did these things to you?

▶ Does it need to be said or done at all?

Read the following examples and indicate whether discrimination (D) or harassment (H) is at play.

_____ A. A supervisor holds regular meetings with his three subordinates, two males and a female. He invariably asks the female to take notes because "her penmanship is better than the males."

_____ B. All minority correctional officers are assigned to the same shift.

_____ C. In scheduling audits, a supervisor sends males to the towns with less desirable hotels because he believes females need more comfortable accommodations.

_____ D. A female's co-workers in the administration office put Playboy "Bunny" posters on the wall of the copy room. She complained to her supervisor that she found the posters offensive, and the posters were taken down. Now her co-workers have begun putting up pictures of nude males in the copy room. She finds the new pictures equally offensive and makes excuses to use the copy machine in another part of the building to avoid seeing the photos.

_____ E. Sheila is constantly putting her arm around Bob's waist when she talks to him in the unit, despite his protests. She jokingly insists that he really likes it. Bob tries to avoid Sheila on the job.

(29)

Sexual Harassment—
Behavior and Conditions (continued)

CONDITIONS

The EEOC guidelines not only define sexual harassment but also specify the conditions that must be present for sexual harassment to exist. The first two conditions are known legally as "quid pro quo" conditions (or something for something), and the third is referred to as a "hostile work environment."

The First Condition

The first condition is that "submission to such conduct is made explicitly or implicitly a term or condition of an individual's employment." This means that a job applicant must submit to a particular activity in order to be hired. For example, sexual harassment occurs when a personnel officer says or implies to a job applicant, "You can have the job if you go out with me."

You probably will not have the responsibility for hiring new officers, so this condition may not apply to you. It is, however, one of the "quid pro quo" conditions of sexual harassment, because something is asked for (sexual conduct) in return for something (a job).

TRUE/FALSE	The first condition of sexual harassment involves submission to a sexual request in order to get the job.
	(32)

III–26 CHAPTER 1: DISCRIMINATION IN THE WORKPLACE

Sexual Harassment—
Behavior and Conditions (continued)

The Second Condition

The second condition is that "submission to or rejection of such conduct by an individual is used as the basis of employment decisions affecting such an individual." This means that decisions you make about an employee's career are based upon whether or not that person submits to your sexual advances.

These career decisions include promotions, training, changes in working conditions and performance evaluations. If you advance or hold back a subordinate, solely because of sexual submission or rejection, this conduct is sexual harassment.

The Third Condition

The third condition is that "such conduct has the purpose or effect of unreasonably interfering with an individual's work performance or creating an intimidating, hostile or offensive working environment."

This condition refers to the climate on the job. If an individual is subjected to dirty jokes, abusive language or leers of a sexual nature that make him uncomfortable or not able to perform well, then that individual is the victim of sexual harassment.

The "hostile work environment" is the most common condition of sexual harassment. While this legal term may sound too harsh, it basically means that you are uncomfortable at your job because of things that your co-workers say or do. For example, Officer Nancy Franklin is married. Officer Jake Henry smiles and winks at her whenever they pass in the hall. He makes it a point to catch her alone at her post and tell her a joke or story with sexual innuendos. She is uncomfortable with this attention but has been unsuccessful in discouraging him. She is being sexually harassed because Henry has created a hostile work environment.

TRUE/FALSE Basing promotions, training or other career advancement decisions on whether an individual submits to or rejects sexual advances is called sexual harassment.
(37)

List the three conditions constituting sexual harassment.

• Relate to _____

• Affect _____

• Create _____
(44)

Sexual Harassment—
Behavior and Conditions (continued)

In summary, conduct with sexual overtones constitutes sexual harassment in the workplace if:

▶ Initial hiring depends upon submission to sexual conduct

▶ Career advancement—i.e., promotions, training opportunities, performance evaluations—depends on submission to sexual conduct

▶ Unwelcome verbal or physical behavior creates a hostile work environment, i.e., the individual is intimidated, under stress or unable to function normally

If the behavior does not meet any of these criteria, it is not sexual harassment. It may be rude and offensive, but it is not illegal.

Sexual Harassment—
Behavior and Conditions (continued)

TRUE/FALSE   Behavior such as telling dirty jokes and showing nude pictures *always* constitutes sexual harassment.

(47)

The following are examples of sexual harassment. Match the EEOC condition with its example.

1. Initial hiring
2. Career advancement
3. Hostile work environment

_____   A. Laurie Anderson's annual performance ratings have always been "outstanding." Lately, her supervisor has been placing his hand on her arm while giving her directions, and she has moved his hand away. Today, he tore up Laurie's training request saying, "If only you were more cooperative, I could do a great deal for your career."

_____   B. Joan Coles was accepted as an apprentice electrician. Joan faces a constant barrage of comments from other workers as she walks from her work location to other areas in the shop. The remarks and gestures range from coarse interjections about female anatomy to specific comments about her figure. Joan is reluctant to move from her station even though she often needs materials from other parts of the shop.

_____   C. Roger Dugan interviewed for an entry level position with Jean Hogan. Jean highly praised Roger's credentials saying he was the most qualified of the applicants. She also commented on Roger's appearance, saying it would be great to have "someone as good looking and well built as you working around here." As a final condition of employment, Jean asked Roger to come to her apartment for an "aptitude test." Dugan refused. He was not offered the job.

(51)

Levels of Harassment

So far, we have been concerned with identifying and defining sex discrimination and sexual harassment. This is the first basic step in learning to deal with it effectively.

Now we will look at the levels of harassment—that is, the relative seriousness of various kinds of prohibited behavior.

Sexual harassment, as we pointed out earlier, is against the law. Those who commit such deeds are subject to a variety of penalties. These penalties range from reprimand by the agency for whom they work, through suspension and removal, to criminal prosecution and imprisonment.

We can divide sexual harassment into four levels. Starting with the least threatening, they are:

▶ Sex role stereotyping

▶ Targeted sexual harassment

▶ Abuse

▶ Criminal behavior

Let's look at each level.

Sexual harassment is against the law.

Levels of Harassment (continued)

SEX ROLE STEREOTYPING

The least threatening level of sexual harassment is *sex role stereotyping*. The key here is that the behavior is not targeted toward a single individual. It stems from traditional thinking or old customs.

For example: the supervisor who calls every female he meets "honey" or "sweetie." Or, the supervisor who says "I'll get my girl to type this after lunch." Such behavior usually is offensive to the recipients.

TARGETED SEXUAL HARASSMENT

At the next level is *targeted sexual harassment*. The conduct here is directed at a specific individual or group.

Some examples are: telling off-color stories to embarrass someone, whistling or making catcalls, brushing against or "accidental" touching. These acts are targeted and intentional toward someone.

These two levels of harassment are most common on the job, and create a hostile work environment. As a supervisor, you need to recognize that there may be intentional or unintentional sexual harassment in your unit. Later in this chapter, we will cover what steps you can take to prevent and eliminate harassment.

In sex role stereotyping, the behavior is not _____ **toward a single individual.**

(41)

An example of _____ **is telling off-color stories intended to embarrass someone.**

(52)

Levels of Harassment (continued)

ABUSE

At the third level is *abuse*. This is sexual harassment that has a serious negative effect on the victim. At this level are threats about job or pay that meet the "quid pro quo" conditions of sexual harassment. Behavior of this type can cause severe stress for the recipient.

An example of abusive behavior would be a supervisor who threatens an employee with a poor performance evaluation if he or she refuses to "put out."

CRIMINAL BEHAVIOR

The most serious type of sexual harassment is classified as *criminal behavior*. This behavior would include violations of the civil or criminal code such as assault and battery, rape, and other sex crimes.

You can see that sexual harassment covers a broad range of conduct, from the unintentional, stereotypical "honey" to major crimes. Overall, the more serious the offense, the more liable the offender is to punishment.

TRUE/FALSE   Threatening someone with an adverse personnel action if he or she doesn't comply with a sexual request is called abuse.

(45)

The most serious types of sexual harassment include violations of the _____

_____.

(61)

Levels of Harassment (continued)

Match the level of harassment with each situation.

1. Sex role stereotyping
2. Targeted sexual harassment
3. Abuse
4. Criminal behavior

_____ A. Mary Jo's co-workers know that she is very modest. They often hide obscene cartoons from magazines in her in-box to make her blush. They laugh when she does.

_____ B. Michael won't assign Cynthia to the night shift in the men's unit because she would be the only female on that shift.

_____ C. Maria tells Roberto that his promotion is all set except for one thing. She offers to tell him about it over dinner.

_____ D. Barbara is attacked at knife point in the stockroom by someone who snuck in the back door and forced her to submit to his advances.

_____ E. Shawn gives the post assignments by saying, "Doreen, honey, I want you to watch the dayroom today."

_____ F. Cheryl gives Alan a little pat on the rear whenever he walks by.

(55)

Responding to Sexual Harassment

Now that you have a better understanding of exactly what sexual harassment is, you can be alert to early signs of it in your unit. If you see a "girlie" calendar in the restroom, or if you hear a sexually or racially-biased joke being told, you can intervene *before* any complaint is made. By quietly talking to your staff, you can make them aware of how important it is to take other people's feelings into consideration. Some officers may not understand that things "we've always done" are no longer acceptable. It is your job to ensure that your subordinates are considerate of one another.

In order to combat sexual harassment, several parties must accept responsibility:

▶ The individual victim must speak up

▶ The victim's supervisor must try to solve the problem and protect the victim, with the support of the agency

▶ In extreme cases, civil and criminal authorities will step in

Let's examine these areas of responsibility in detail.

Individual Responsibility

If you believe that you are a victim of sexual harassment, you should take the first step in stopping the unwanted behavior. Tell your harasser that you find his* actions offensive. Keep the conversation brief, and private; do not give mixed messages by smiling, or joking about the situation. Be direct, and firm. Use sentences such as "Please do not touch me when we pass in the hall," or "I will gladly discuss the post assignments, but I'm not interested in having dinner with you."

Confronting the harasser is a difficult thing to do. Most victims of sexual harassment are reluctant to talk about their experience or feelings. They fear being seen as a troublemaker, as too sensitive or not "one of the guys." In addition, the perceptions that men and women have of what constitutes sexual harassment are vastly different. A recent poll asked men and women workers how they would respond to sexual advances on the job. Of the men, 75% said they would be flattered, while 15% would be offended. Among the women, 75% said they would be offended.

In cases of sex role stereotyping, it is especially important that the recipient speak up. Very often, the harasser is simply following family or community tradition in the treatment of the opposite sex, and is unaware that the behavior is offensive to others.

If you are the victim of sex role stereotyping, tell the harasser that you are bothered by what he says or does. Ask the harasser to rethink his treatment of the opposite sex. It will not be easy for the harasser to overcome a lifetime of unconscious habit, but you must make him aware of the problem.

The same first step is appropriate if you are the victim of targeted sexual harassment. Confront the harasser and explain that his behavior is unwelcome; ask that he stop the behavior. If you do not speak up, the alleged harasser can legitimately claim that he was unaware that his conduct was offensive. You must assert your right to be free of any conduct of a sexual nature that makes you uncomfortable.

If talking to your harasser does not change his behavior toward you, write him a letter. Be specific about what behavior you find offensive, and why. Tell him what action you plan to take next if his harassment doesn't stop. Your copy of this letter is important evidence if you choose to file a formal sexual harassment charge.

---

*We realize that both men and women are victims of sexual harassment. For the purposes of simplifying the language in this chapter, however, we will use "he" as the harasser and "she" as the victim.

Individual Responsibility (continued)

Once you have made your harasser aware that his behavior is unwelcome, it becomes his responsibility to respect your request to stop. Ideally, he will no longer say sexist things or indulge in conduct that you find offensive. In real life, however, people who engage in sexual harassment often don't behave according to accepted norms.

If you are the target of sexual abuse, for example, confronting your harasser is likely to have little effect. Someone who threatens you with a poor performance evaluation if you don't submit to sexual conduct is probably not going to suddenly change his behavior at your request. Regardless of the circumstances, however, make your feelings of stress and unhappiness clear to your harasser.

If you continue to be sexually harassed, you may have to take additional measures. The next step is to inform your supervisor of the problem. If your harasser *is* your supervisor, approach his superior. You may contact this superior either in person or in writing. Now it becomes the responsibility of the organization to deal with the situation.

If you are the victim of rape, or assault and battery while on the job, notify the police and your supervisor at once. This act of criminal behavior must be handled by criminal authorities.

TRUE/FALSE   The victim of sexual harassment should first confront the harasser, making it clear that the behavior is unwelcome.

(21)

TRUE/FALSE   Once the victim of sexual harassment has confronted the harasser and told him to stop the offensive behavior, the matter will end there.

(27)

If the victim of sexual harassment receives no satisfaction after confronting the harasser, the next step is to inform

_____.

(31)

The Supervisor's Responsibility

Your responsibility in cases of sexual harassment involving two of your subordinates includes taking positive steps to correct the grievance, protecting the victim while looking into the complaint, and counseling the harasser. As a supervisor, you represent the organization, and the responsibility for dealing with sexual harassment complaints starts with you. Throughout the process, your actions should be guided by your facility's policies and procedures.

Your first step in resolving the grievance is to investigate the complaint. Talk to the victim, privately, of course, and obtain the facts of the case. Then talk to the alleged harasser, and get the other side of the story. It may be difficult for you to determine the truth if one party accuses another, the other denies it, and there is no evidence available. Be as calm and reasonable as you can be in your investigation. Interview all witnesses to the harassment. Thoroughly document all the information you collect, including the statements by the accuser, the accused, and any witnesses.

During the investigation, you should:

- Do your best to maintain the confidentiality of all parties
- Protect the accuser from retaliation
- Be sure to investigate the complaint and come to a decision promptly

The issue of sexual harassment is a sensitive and an emotional one. Both parties need to slow down and work through their emotions—anger, resentment, worry and so forth. You should stress to each individual how important it is that all staff feel comfortable in the work environment. You also should state that, as a supervisor, you will strive to achieve this goal. When appropriate, you should suggest professional counseling for the accuser and/or the accused.

If you feel the charge is substantiated (by evidence), you must explain the consequences to the harasser if he or she continues the poor behavior.

The Supervisor's Responsibility (continued)

If you are not successful in ending the harassment, the victim can then file a formal complaint. When this happens, EEOC and correctional officials must investigate. During the formal grievance investigation and appeal process, the agency and, in particular, the supervisor, assumes the responsibility not only to investigate the incident but also to protect the victim from any retaliation for filing the complaint. This retaliation may take the form of threats at home by the harasser, or a general coldness on the part of co-workers toward the victim.

While the investigation process is taking place, it is likely that the accuser will not come to work. While this makes it easier to prevent retaliation, you will need to re-arrange the work schedule.

In addition to preventing retaliation, you also must ensure that the victim's career is not affected. You cannot penalize the victim for taking leave while the investigation is proceeding. Moreover, you cannot give the victim an unsatisfactory rating on her performance appraisal.

Different agencies have different penalties established for sexual harassment cases. Persons found guilty of continued harassment are penalized based on the severity of the harassment and the number of offenses of which they are guilty. Check with your superior or the policy manual for your facility to determine what penalties apply.

List the supervisor's responsibilities in sexual harassment cases.

- _____
- _____
- _____
- _____

(34)

The Role of Outside Authorities

When an act of sexual harassment reaches the level of serious abuse or criminal behavior, such as assault and battery or rape, then civil and criminal authorities assume primary responsibility.

At this time, the organization still has a responsibility to the victim. While the harasser may be found guilty by a court and be subject to the penalties of law, these penalties do nothing for the victim. As the victim's supervisor, you should be sensitive to the hurt the victim has suffered. Be sure that you work with her to ease her return to work.

In the case of assault or rape, outside civil and criminal authorities assume responsibility.

Sexual Harassment—Responsibility

Awareness of what sexual harassment is will help you avoid it in your daily interaction with your staff. But, try as you might to prevent it from happening, you may be guilty yourself of sexual harassment. Here are three suggestions to help you avoid being accused of harassment.

Stick to the boundaries and guidelines your agency has set. Don't think that a person or situation is an "exception to the rule." The policy at your facility is probably clear—if your action is perceived as harassing, embarrassing or threatening, address it immediately.

If you suspect that *your* actions have offended someone, *ask the other person* about it right then and there. The longer you delay, the stickier the situation will get. Ask your questions in a non-threatening way: "Did I do something that made you feel uncomfortable?" Then be quiet and listen. Ask a follow-up question: "Is there anything else you would like to say?" and use your IPC skills to really hear what the answer is. Even if your actions did not offend the person, you should still express your regrets. You might say, "If I offended you in any way, please accept my apology." Of course, be sincere.

If you think the situation might come back to haunt you, *tell your superior.* You can simply say, "I made a mistake, and here's what I did to correct it." It won't hurt to make him or her aware of a situation that may come up later.

What are three things that the victim of sexual harassment should do?

_____

_____

_____

(50)

List three things you should do to make sure that you are not guilty of sexual harassment.

- Stick to _____

- _____ the other person

- Report to your _____

(46)

Responsibility—Review

Let's summarize the areas of responsibility in responding to and stopping sexual harassment in the workplace.

Individual

- Must first confront the harasser and ask him/her to stop the unwelcome behavior.
- If confrontation is not effective, must report the matter to his/her supervisor.
- If the supervisor is the harasser, must report the matter to next level superior.
- If the problem is not solved by the supervisor, should file a formal complaint to the EEOC.

Supervisor (Organization)

- Should take active steps to prevent sexual harassment from occurring.
- Must investigate the complaint and counsel the harasser.
- If a formal complaint is filed, must assist the EEOC and management officials in the investigation.
- Must protect the victim from any retaliation for filing the complaint.
- Must discipline the harasser as appropriate.

Civil and Criminal Authorities

- Assume primary responsibility when an act of sexual harassment reaches the level of serious abuse, or when it is criminal behavior, such as assault, battery or rape.

Review

List the three persons/organizations responsible for seeing that sexual harassment does not take place and for seeing that guilty parties are punished.

- _____

- _____

- _____

(39)

TRUE/FALSE The individual must assert his or her own right to be free of any unwanted sexual behavior.

(42)

List three actions that you, as a supervisor, can take to respond to and stop sexual harassment in your unit.

- _____

- _____

- _____

(66)

If you are not successful in your efforts to stop sexual harassment in your unit, then the victim can take the next step; he or she can file a _____.

(53)

If the sexual harassment becomes criminal behavior, _____ must assume responsibility.

(57)

Persons found guilty of sexual harassment will be penalized based on two factors:

- _____

- _____

(60)

Sexual Harassment—Case Study

Read the "Tom and Janice" case study carefully and answer the questions at the end of each segment.

BACKGROUND:

Tom enjoys his role as office clown. One of the things he likes to do is to tell risqué stories to one of his male co-workers in a loud enough voice so that the females in the unit can hear it. At the punch line, he and his friend laugh loudly while, at the same time, they watch how the women react. Most of the women pretend not to hear the stories; some are amused and react with coy smiles. Janice, on the other hand, is offended and feels degraded. She hasn't said anything to Tom, however.

Is this sexual harassment?

☐ Yes   ☐ No

Why or why not?

_____
_____
_____
_____
_____

Should anyone else get involved?

☐ Yes   ☐ No

Why or why not?

_____
_____
_____
_____
_____

(63)

CHAPTER 1: DISCRIMINATION IN THE WORKPLACE   III—43

Sexual Harassment—
Case Study (continued)

Suppose Janice tells Tom that the stories upset her and make it hard for her to do her job. Tom responds by laughing. The next time he tells his stories, he makes sure Janice is nearby to hear them.

What should Janice do now?

_____
_____
_____
_____

What should Janice's supervisor do?

_____
_____
_____
_____

(67)

Suppose Janice's supervisor tells her not to be prudish, that "boys will be boys," and she'll have to put up with Tom like everyone else does.

What can Janice do to assert her rights?

_____
_____
_____
_____

(70)

Providing a Harassment-free Workplace

All managers and supervisors have a responsibility to provide a positive work environment. This means that you must take active measures to ensure a workplace free from harassment.

Your two primary responsibilities in providing a harassment-free environment are:

▶ Prevention

▶ Elimination

We will examine these responsibilities in the next few pages.

TRUE/FALSE It is never permissible to treat people differently.
(49)

The law requires that employment decisions be based on things other than _____, _____, _____ **or religion.**
(54)

The supervisor's responsibilities in providing a workplace free of sexual harassment include:

• _____

• _____

(62)

Providing a Harassment-free Workplace (continued)

PREVENTION

Prevention through education and awareness is perhaps the most effective method of ensuring a harassment-free work environment. Alert your subordinates to the rights of all employees to work in a harassment-free climate. Explain the definition of sexual harassment to your staff. Tell them how much damage a charge of sexual harassment does to the morale of a unit, and the physical and mental pain it can cause the victim. Make them aware of the penalties that will be taken against harassers.

Awareness also is a key part in enabling you to provide a good working climate. If you are aware of what is going on in your unit—the interaction between your subordinates and between the officers and the inmates—you can quickly prevent small hassles from becoming big problems. Use your IPC skills to observe what is really happening. Do the men and women sit on opposite sides of the room during staff meetings? Are the female officers reluctant to voice their opinions? Have you heard derogatory remarks about "men" or "women"? Are there one or two of your subordinates who don't mingle with the rest of the unit?

Your steps to prevent sexual harassment will indicate your agency's commitment to the goal of eliminating sex discrimination.

Two ways to prevent sexual harassment are through _____ **and** _____ .

(58)

The most effective way of ensuring a harassment-free work environment is through _____ **your staff.**

(69)

Providing a Harassment-free Workplace (continued)

ELIMINATION

The task of eliminating sexual harassment falls on all managers and supervisors within the organization. By doing your job well, you set the tone in your unit. If you exhibit professional, businesslike conduct—and show that you expect it from your staff—the workplace probably will be free of discrimination and harrassment probably will be eliminated from the workplace.

When minor incidents of sexual harassment *do* occur, you should thoroughly investigate all the charges. Be objective—you're trying to find out what happened. Try not to be defensive about the situation, as if the charge is a personal reflection on your supervisory skills. Don't be overly aggressive—intimidating and scaring your subordinates. You then may never get the whole story.

It is in the interest of all the parties—the organization, the victim, and the harasser—that minor complaints be handled informally by you, the victim's immediate supervisor. You can usually get the harasser to stop the offensive behavior, especially if you appear fair and even-handed. Most instances of sexual harassment can be eliminated in this way.

"Minor complaints" might include:

▶ A male officer calling all females "honey"

▶ A male officer telling a "dirty" joke in the presence of a female officer

▶ An inmate complaining about an officer touching him

TRUE/FALSE   It is in the best interest of all parties that minor complaints be investigated by the supervisor.
(73)

Providing a Harassment-free Workplace—Review

Check the statements that are true.

_____ A. If supervisors set a professional, business-like tone in the workplace, it will generally be observed by employees.

_____ B. When employees feel they have been the victims of sexual harassment, they should not stir up any trouble for anyone.

_____ C. The organization must not only investigate the complaint but also protect the victim from retaliation.

_____ D. When minor breaches of norms do occur, supervisors should approach the situation aggressively.

_____ E. If outside authorities are involved in a case, the organization is relieved of all responsibility.

_____ F. The organization has a responsibility to the victims to correct their grievances through restitution of back pay, and so forth.

(26)

Case Study

JERRY HILL CASE STUDY

Jerry Hill, an African American officer, has just come into your office and is complaining about "jokes" being made in the lunchroom. He indicates that while the white officers seem friendly enough in the workplace, he finds "jokes" about large lips, short curly hair and skin color offensive.

You have heard these "jokes" also. They've been told for years, but Hill is the first person to complain. You believe Hill is serious about being offended, but you also think that the people telling the "jokes" don't mean any harm.

Is this discrimination or harassment and why?

(56)

Is there any legal violation and why?

(59)

What would be your response to Hill and why?

(65)

Case Study

JANE DAVIS CASE STUDY

Jane Davis, a female officer, has just come to your office complaining about being sexually harassed. Davis, who has been with the department for one year, is competitive and aggressive in her dealings with male staff members. You personally know she has never had any problems in voicing her opinions to her co-workers.

Davis' complaint is that John Milos, a co-worker, has been particularly vile and offensive of late. Specifically, over the past two months he has repeatedly used "sexual talk" around her even when she has told him she doesn't like it. On a couple of occasions, he put his arm around her shoulder or waist, which she promptly removed. Today was the final straw. He asked her into his office and showed her several pictures of males and females in sexual activity, including some with animals. Davis claims this activity is starting to affect her work.

Is this discrimination or harassment and why?

_____

_____

_____

_____

(64)

Putting aside the obscene materials part, is there any legal violation and why?

_____

_____

_____

_____

(72)

Case Study

ROXANNE ROST CASE STUDY

You've known Roxanne Rost since high school, where you played on the field hockey team together. After you became a correctional officer, you convinced Roxanne that it was a great career. You and Roxanne worked together as line officers for six years. Last year, you were promoted, and now you supervise Roxanne. You're still good friends, and are in the same bowling league.

Yesterday, you noticed that Officer Dean Jakes looked very upset as he left for the day. His post assignment had been the guard tower, with Officer Rost. You noticed that Roxanne had a slight smirk on her face. You thought you would ask Roxanne what happened tonight, while you're bowling together.

What should you do?

_____
_____
_____
_____

What should you say to Rost? _____
_____
_____
_____
_____

What should you say to Jakes?
_____
_____
_____
_____

(68)

Summary

Let's review what was covered in this chapter.

▶ Some of the social forces in recent years that have changed the way we do business in the workplace and that have made all employers, including governments, more sensitive to the rights of individual workers are:

— The Civil Rights Movement

— The Women's Movement

— The increased number of females in the workforce

— The increased number of females as heads of households, therefore needing equal pay, not just a second income

— A concern for the disabled

— Increased cultural pride in minority groups, demanding better treatment

— More unionization among government workers

▶ Equal Employment Opportunity (EEO) laws are legislative measures designed to protect the rights of citizens in the workplace.

▶ EEO laws affect all facets of employment, including:

— Recruitment

— Selection

— Compensation

— Discipline

— Treatment

▶ Laws/amendments passed to protect citizens from discrimination include:

— Fifth Amendment, U.S. Constitution, 1791

— Fourteenth Amendment, U.S. Constitution, 1868

— Civil Rights Act of 1964, amended by EEO Act of 1972

— The Age Discrimination Act of 1967

— The Rehabilitation Act of 1973

— The Americans with Disabilities Act of 1990

— The Civil Rights Act of 1991

— The Family and Medical Leave Act of 1993

Summary (continued)

- Discrimination is a broad term defined as "differential treatment." Harassment is a very specific form of sex discrimination.

- One of the following conditions must be present for sexual harassment to exist:
  - The first condition is that "submission to such conduct is made explicitly or implicitly a term or condition of an individual's employment" (*quid pro quo*).
  - The second condition is that "submission to or rejection of such conduct by an individual is used as the basis of employment decisions affecting such an individual" (*quid pro quo*).
  - The third condition is that "such conduct has the purpose or effect of unreasonably interfering with an individual's work performance or creating an intimidating, hostile or offensive working environment" (hostile work environment).

- The range of acts that can be defined as sexual harassment are:
  - Sex role stereotyping
  - Targeted sexual harassment
  - Abuse
  - Criminal behavior

- As a supervisor, your primary responsibilities for providing a workplace free from harassment are:
  - Prevention
  - Elimination

Answer Key—Discrimination in the Workplace

1. The laws that protect citizens from discrimination include:
   - Fifth Amendment, 1791
   - Fourteenth Amendment, 1868
   - Civil Rights Act, 1964—amended by EEO Act, 1972
   - The Age Discrimination Act, 1967
   - The Rehabilitation Act, 1973
   - The Americans with Disabilities Act, 1990
   - The Civil Rights Act, 1991
   - The Family and Medical Leave Act, 1993

2. The ADA affects the areas of **employment** and **access.**

3. The goal of the "Glass Ceiling Act" is to increase the number of women and minorities in **management and decision-making** positions.

4. The examples of discrimination are:
   - ✓ A. Not hiring a 40-year-old man who is qualified
   - ___ B. Not hiring a woman even though she is unqualified
   - ✓ C. Asking women questions not asked of men during an employment interview
   - ✓ D. Not promoting a person who is near retirement age

5. The Fifth Amendment covers actions by the federal government, including the government as the **employer.**

6. The ADA prohibits discrimination against **persons with physical or mental disabilities.**

Answer Key—Discrimination in the Workplace (continued)

7. The social forces that have changed the workplace include:
   - The Civil Rights Movement
   - The Women's Movement
   - The increased number of women in the workforce
   - The increased number of female heads of households
   - A concern for the disabled
   - The increasingly culturally diverse workforce
   - More unionization among government workers

8. Sexual harassment is a specific form of **sex discrimination**.

9. The Fifth Amendment states that no person shall be deprived of **life, liberty** or **property** without due process.

10. The EEO laws are intended to **assure equal treatment of all workers, those from majority as well as minority groups**.

11. The EEOC defined sexual harassment as "uninvited conduct with **sexual overtones** in the workplace."

12. The Family and Medical Leave Act allows an employee to take up to **12 weeks** of unpaid leave for a family or medical emergency.

13. **False.** While the Fifth and Fourteenth Amendments contain the same basic prohibition, the Fifth Amendment refers to the federal government as the employer and the Fourteenth Amendment applies to state and local governments.

14. EEO laws affect all areas of employment, including:
    - Recruitment
    - Selection
    - Compensation
    - Discipline
    - Treatment

Answer Key—Discrimination in the Workplace (continued)

15. **False.** You can't ask women questions that you don't ask men. This is sex discrimination.

16. **True.** The EEOC has said that discrimination on the basis of gender includes sexual harassment.

17. **False.** Neither the Fifth nor the Fourteenth Amendments are used very often in discrimination or harassment lawsuits. The Civil Rights Act of 1964 is more specific, and is most often cited in lawsuits.

18. **True.** The basic principle of the EEO laws is that employees should be treated as individuals, not as members of a group.

19. **False.** A male supervisor asking a female officer for a date might be just a normal male-female interaction. It would be sexual harassment if a hiring or promotion decision were based on the invitation.

20. Title VII of the Civil Rights Act prohibits **discrimination,** and therefore sexual **harassment.**

21. **True.** The victim of perceived sexual harassment must make sure that the harasser is aware that his or her behavior is unwelcome.

22. **False.** It is not only the law but also a good supervisory technique to make work-related decisions based on a person's merits.

23. **False.** The Family and Medical Leave Act allows workers to take up to 12 weeks of unpaid leave—for medical or family emergencies—without penalty.

24. The Fifth Amendment covers the employment rights of **federal** workers, while the Fourteenth Amendment protects the rights of **state and local** employees.

25. **True.** More and more charges of sexual harassment are being filed, and more and more time and money is being spent as a result of this controversial issue.

Answer Key—Discrimination in the Workplace (continued)

26. The true statements are:

    ✓ A. If supervisors set a professional, business-like tone in the workplace, it will generally be observed by employees.

    ___ B. When employees feel they have been the victims of sexual harassment, they should not stir up any trouble for anyone.

    ✓ C. The organization must not only investigate the complaint but also protect the victim from retaliation.

    ___ D. When minor breaches of norms do occur, supervisors should approach the situation aggressively.

    ___ E. If outside authorities are involved in a case, the organization is relieved of all responsibility.

    ✓ F. The organization has a responsibility to the victims to correct their grievances through restitution of back pay and so forth.

27. **False.** Ideally, the harasser will stop harassing the victim. Very often, however, people who engage in sexual harassment don't behave according to accepted norms.

28. The Civil Rights Act applies to:

    - Private employers with 15 or more employees
    - State and local government employers
    - Unions
    - Employment agencies

Answer Key—Discrimination in the Workplace (continued)

29. In the examples, **D** indicates discrimination and **H** indicates harassment:

    __D__ A. This is differential treatment based on sex.

    __D__ B. This is an example of race/ethnic discrimination, because the officers are assigned based on their race and/or ethnic background.

    __D__ C. This is sex discrimination based on gender. The supervisor is treating females preferentially based on an assumption about them that has no bearing on job responsibilities.

    __H__ D. This is an example of sexual harassment. There are obvious sexual overtones from the pictures. Further, the pictures are "unwelcome," an important element in the definition of sexual harassment.

    __H__ E. This is sexual harassment. It is unwelcome physical conduct that affects Bob's work environment and job performance.

30. **False.** Both men and women experience sexual harassment in the workplace.

31. If the victim of sexual harassment receives no satisfaction after confronting the harasser, the next step is to inform **the supervisor.**

32. **True.** One of the quid pro quo conditions of sexual harassment is that a job applicant must submit to a particular activity to be hired.

33. The **Bill of Rights** was the first legislation to protect citizens' rights in the United States.

34. A supervisor's responsibilities in cases of sexual harassment include:
    - Be alert to possible problems before they occur
    - Investigate the complaint
    - Take positive steps to correct the grievance
    - Protect the victim
    - Counsel the harasser
    - Maintain confidentiality
    - Investigate and come to a conclusion promptly

Answer Key—Discrimination in the Workplace (continued)

35. The Civil Rights Act prohibits employment discrimination based on **race, color, religion, sex** or national origin.

36. The true statements are:

    √ A. Harassers may be both supervisors and co-workers.

    √ B. Sexual harassment is part of sex discrimination.

    ___ C. The Civil Rights Act of 1964 prohibited discrimination based on merit.

    ___ D. Although sex discrimination is against the law, sexual harassment is not.

    √ E. The Civil Rights Act of 1964 is the major legislation cited in discrimination lawsuits.

    √ F. Sexual harassment not only violates individual rights but it also represents a huge dollar drain to lost productivity and legal fees.

37. **True.** This is the second quid pro quo condition of sexual harassment.

38. **False.** Laws have been on the books since 1791, and through the years more legislation was passed making it clearer that discrimination was prohibited. Unfortunately, many of these laws were not actively enforced until the 1900s.

39. The three persons/organizations responsible for seeing that sexual harassment does not take place and for seeing that guilty parties are disciplined are:

    - The individual victim
    - The victim's supervisor and the organization for which the victim works
    - In extreme cases, civil and criminal authorities

40. The Age Discrimination Act applies to persons between the ages of **40** and **70**.

41. In sex role stereotyping, the behavior is not **targeted** toward a single individual.

42. **True.** Responsibility in resolving cases of sexual harassment begins with the individual who is subjected to the unwanted behavior.

43. Discrimination is defined as "**differential treatment.**"

Answer Key—Discrimination in the Workplace (continued)

44. The three conditions constituting sexual harassment are:
    - Relate **to initial hiring**
    - Affect **career advancement**
    - Create **a hostile work environment**

45. **True.** Abuse involves threats about job or pay.

46. Three things you should do to make sure that you are not guilty of sexual harassment are:
    - Stick to **the boundaries**
    - **Ask** the other person
    - Report to your **superior**

47. **False.** Such behavior is considered sexual harassment if it is unwelcomed by the recipient.

48. Showing favoritism toward or bias against an employee because of his or her gender is called **sex discrimination.**

49. **False.** It is permissible to treat people differently *based on seniority or merit.*

50. Some of the things that the victim of sexual harassment should do include:
    - Confront the harasser and ask him or her to stop the unwelcome behavior
    - Report the matter to his or her supervisor, if confronting the harasser has no effect
    - If the supervisor *is* the harasser, report the matter to the next level superior
    - If the problem cannot be solved by the supervisor or superior, file a formal complaint with the EEOC

Answer Key—Discrimination in the Workplace (continued)

51. In the examples of sexual harassment, the following EEOC conditions apply:

    __2__ A. (Career advancement)

    __3__ B. (Hostile work environment)

    __1__ C. (Initial hiring)

52. An example of **targeted sexual harassment** is telling off-color stories to embarrass someone.

53. If you are not successful in your efforts to stop sexual harassment in your unit, then the victim can take the next step; he or she can file a **formal complaint.**

54. The law requires that employment decisions be based on things other than **color, sex, race** or religion.

55. Match the level of harassment with each situation.

    1. Sex role stereotyping
    2. Targeted sexual harassment
    3. Abuse
    4. Criminal behavior

    __2__ A. Her co-workers are intentionally and deliberately embarrassing her for their own satisfaction. The key here is that they are doing something to her that they are not doing to other employees.

    __1__ B. While this might seem as if the behavior is aimed at Cynthia, Michael is actually stereotyping women. He is assuming that she would be uncomfortable by being the only female on the shift.

    __3__ C. Maria, the supervisor, seems to be requiring non-job related activity (appearing at her place) as a condition of the promotion. The sexual innuendo seems clear. If Roberto loses the promotion as a result of his refusal, this may be abuse.

    __4__ D. She is a victim of assault, which is a criminal act and a violation of the criminal code. The perpetrator would be subject to prosecution by the authorities.

    __1__ E. Shawn is guilty of sex role stereotyping by calling Doreen, and possibly every woman, "honey."

    __2__ F. Alan is the victim of targeted sexual harassment.

Answer Key—Discrimination in the Workplace (continued)

56. This is discrimination based on race because the "jokes" show bias against a person because of his race.

57. If the sexual harassment becomes criminal behavior, **outside authorities** must assume responsibility.

58. Two ways to prevent sexual harassment are through **education** and **awareness.**

59. Yes, there is a legal violation. Courts have held that persistent jokes or comments that downgrade a person because of race, color, religion, national origin or sex, violate Title VII of the Civil Rights Act of 1964.

60. Persons found guilty of sexual harassment will be penalized based on two factors:
    - Severity of offense
    - Number of offenses

61. The most serious types of sexual harassment include violations of the **civil or criminal code.**

62. The supervisor's responsibilities in providing a workplace free of sexual harassment include:
    - Prevention
    - Elimination

63. No. If no one hearing the stories finds them offensive, then telling them does not constitute sexual harassment. Janice is responsible for telling Tom that the stories bother her and that they are unwelcome. But, as a supervisor, if you hear the stories, you might tell Tom that others might be offended, and that he should make sure his audience is receptive.

    Yes, Tom is engaging in sex role stereotyping. His conduct is untargeted because he seems to be playing to all the females, not anyone in particular. Once Janice asserts her right and tells Tom, the responsibility shifts. It is then Tom's responsibility to respect her right, and the organization's responsibility to protect it.

64. This is sexual harassment because it is uninvited conduct with sexual overtones in the workplace. Also, it appears that this situation may be interfering with Jane's work performance.

Answer Key—Discrimination in the Workplace (continued)

65. Your response to Hill might include the following actions:
    - Reaffirm your commitment to a discrimination-free environment
    - Talk personally to those involved in the "jokes," explaining to them how offensive they are, not only to Hill but also to you
    - Discuss the policy statement about offensive and abusive language
    - Be prepared to take disciplinary action if the "jokes" continue

66. Activities that you, as a supervisor, can do to stop sexual harassment include:
    - Take active steps to prevent harassment from occurring
    - Investigate complaints of sexual harassment
    - Counsel the harasser
    - Assist EEOC and management officials in the investigation if a formal complaint is filed
    - Protect the victim from retaliation
    - Discipline the harasser as appropriate

67. Janice should report the matter to her supervisor. The supervisor then should try to resolve the problem by explaining the situation, and the consequences, to Tom.

68. The event you observed should alert you that there *may* be a problem. Don't assume there is, however, until you have a chance to talk to the parties involved.

    Informally, ask Officer Rost how everything went during the day. You might mention that Officer Jakes looked upset and that you were concerned.

    Also, informally ask Officer Jakes if there was a problem during his tour at the guard tower. There could be many reasons for what you observed, so don't jump to conclusions. See if he wants to talk but don't press the issue.

69. The most effective way of ensuring a harassment-free work environment is through **educating** your staff.

Answer Key—Discrimination in the Workplace (continued)

70. If informal procedures do not solve the problem, Janice can file a formal complaint. The supervisor and the agency have clear responsibilities in responding to formal complaints. After Janice files a formal complaint, EEOC and supervisory officials must investigate it, and the organization must protect Janice from any retaliation. If Tom is found guilty of harassment, the agency will discipline Tom and compensate Janice in some way. For example, if the harassment resulted in an adverse job action against Janice, her job would be reinstated with back pay. Each case will have a different resolution and compensation.

71. Match the following legislation to its measure/effect/requirement.

    1. Fifth Amendment, 1791
    2. Fourteenth Amendment, 1868
    3. Civil Rights Act, 1964
    4. Age Discrimination Act, 1967
    5. Americans with Disabilities Act, 1990
    6. Civil Rights Act, 1991
    7. Family and Medical Leave Act, 1993

    __4__ A. Prohibits discrimination against 60-year-old workers

    __6__ B. Encourages moving women into management positions

    __3__ C. Prohibits employment based on religion

    __2__ D. States that no state shall deprive any person of life, liberty or property without due process, nor deny equal protection of the law

    __7__ E. Allows extra, unpaid leave for emergencies

    __3__ F. Prohibits membership discrimination based on race

    __5__ G. Prohibits discrimination against individuals with physical and mental handicaps

72. Putting aside the obscene materials, there is a potential legal violation. Sexual harassment that causes an oppressive work environment, even if there is no loss of tangible job benefits, has been held illegal under Title VII. A "hostile work environment" is a very common problem.

73. **True.** Many small sexual harassment problems can be resolved at the unit level with timely and careful intervention by supervisors.

CHAPTER 2

Civil Liability in Corrections

Objectives

At the end of this chapter, you will be able to:

▶ Explain the three types of civil lawsuits inmates file.
▶ List the three degrees of fault in tort actions.
▶ List the three forms of relief in tort suits.
▶ List the three types of damages available in a civil suit.
▶ Explain inmates rights in regard to searches.
▶ Define use of force.
▶ Explain how reasonableness and necessity are factors involved in use of force.
▶ Define deliberate indifference in regard to an inmate's medical or mental health care.
▶ Define conditions of confinement.
▶ Explain inmates' rights in regard to access to the legal system.
▶ Give examples of inmate's rights in regard to freedom of religion, speech and press.
▶ Define indemnification.
▶ List four of the seven steps that help prevent personal liability.

Introduction

Lawsuits have become a way of life in the 90's. It's hard to read the newspaper without finding a story about someone who is being sued, and corrections is not exempt. Staff may file lawsuits over discrimination in the workplace. And, inmates may file suits against officers, supervisors and superintendents.

Many supervisors, therefore, are worried about being sued and being found liable for a large sum of money. They fear that even an innocent mistake could turn into a disaster.

As a correctional supervisor, you *do* need to be concerned about lawsuits—but in a healthy, constructive way. You need to be aware of and sensitive to the concerns that the courts have singled out. You also need to know your agency's policies and procedures well. Only then will you be able to fulfill your supervisory responsibilities without the fear of lawsuits.

Chapter 1 of this book focused on discrimination in the workplace, the topic of lawsuits brought by staff. In this chapter we will focus on lawsuits brought by *inmates*. We will give you an overview of civil law and explore how you and your staff can avoid liability in inmate lawsuits.

TRUE/FALSE   Both inmates and staff have rights that are protected by the courts.

(6)

Increasing/Decreasing   The number of lawsuits in the United States is _____.

(9)

Two ways that you can reduce your fear about lawsuits are:

- _____
- _____

(12)

Criminal Law

Our law is divided into two categories: criminal law and civil law. Let's take a brief look at each of them.

In criminal cases, people are accused of committing crimes against the *public*—even though there may be only one victim. State or federal *government* representatives, therefore, prosecute the accused.

During the criminal proceedings, the victims (if any are involved) are not formal parties in the case. This means that they may serve as witnesses and testify against the accused, but they cannot receive compensation for their injuries.

If the judges or juries believe the accused are guilty beyond a reasonable doubt (roughly 95% certainty), they are convicted of the crimes. Conviction can lead to imprisonment, a fine or some other penalty. Any monies collected from fines go to the government.

Convicted persons may appeal their sentences.

Let's look at an example. Suppose Myron Cooper sells a pound of cocaine to an undercover police officer. Unfortunately for Myron, there are state laws against possessing and selling illegal drugs. He is charged with breaking those laws and brought to trial.

Myron is prosecuted by the state representative. After weighing the evidence, the jury decides that he is guilty beyond a reasonable doubt. The judge sentences him to the state correctional facility.

All the inmates in your facility have either been charged with or convicted of criminal offenses.

TRUE/FALSE   Criminal cases are considered crimes against the public.

(15)

Do/Do not   Victims in criminal cases _____ receive compensation for their injuries.

(19)

TRUE/FALSE   In a criminal proceeding, the prosecutor represents the individual victim of the crime.

(23)

Civil Law

Civil law pertains to the private rights of individuals and the legal proceedings connected with these rights. For example, take the case of divorce. It is not a criminal matter because there is no crime against the public. Rather, divorce is a civil matter involving the private rights of two individuals.

Private citizens usually bring civil suits, rather than the government. They are formal parties in the suit and are referred to as the *plaintiffs*. We call those accused of some harmful action *defendants*.

Lawyers for both sides argue the cases before the courts. Judges or juries decide the cases based on a preponderance of the evidence (more than 50% certainty of guilt), rather than the "beyond a reasonable doubt" standard used in criminal cases. If the plaintiffs win, they receive monetary or some other type of awards.

Civil lawsuits are the focus of this chapter.

Match the following.

1. Plaintiff
2. Defendant
3. Civil law
4. Criminal law

_____ A. The "victim" of wrongful actions

_____ B. The person accused of a wrongful action(s)

_____ C. Cases decided on the basis of a preponderance of the evidence

_____ D. The government fulfills this role in criminal cases

(1)

Match the following.

1. Civil case
2. Criminal case

_____ A. Sex discrimination

_____ B. Assault

_____ C. Bank robbery

_____ D. Drug trafficking

_____ E. Slander

_____ F. Cruel and unusual punishment

_____ G. Freedom of religion

_____ H. Sexual harassment

(4)

Inmate Lawsuits

As a correctional supervisor, you are responsible for ensuring that your staff carry out their duty to protect inmates' rights, including their right to be reasonably safe. This does not mean that you constantly have to watch your subordinates. Instead, proper supervision is often the key to avoiding liability from many inmate lawsuits.

In this section, we will review the three common types of civil lawsuits brought by inmates against correctional staff.

▶ Tort suits—an inmate claims that he or she has suffered an injury because of the fault of one or more staff members. For example, an inmate claims that he lost sight in one eye because a correctional officer failed to inspect a compressor, which later exploded.

▶ Civil rights actions—an inmate (or inmates) alleges that one or more staff and/or the facility have violated his or her constitutional rights. For example, several inmates at a facility claim that inadequate living conditions violate their right to be free from cruel and unusual punishment.

▶ State constitutional rights actions—an inmate (or inmates) alleges that one or more staff and/or the facility have violated his or her *state* constitutional rights. For example, suppose a state law says that no correctional facility can exceed its design capacity. Several inmates claim that their state right is being violated because the facility they're housed in is over its limit.

An inmate claiming a violation of her First Amendment right of free speech would file a _____ suit.
(8)

An inmate claiming a staff member caused his leg injury would file a _____ suit.
(13)

Tort Suits

People file tort suits when they feel that they have been injured because of the fault of other persons. In this type of suit, a person often claims that the person at fault acted negligently. In a tort case, the injury does not have to refer to an actual physical injury, like a broken leg. The person can claim he suffered harm because of a threat or mental pain.

Tort suits are typically filed in state courts. In the correctional setting, tort actions commonly focus on such issues as:

▶ The loss of an inmate's belongings

▶ An officer using racial terms when referring to an inmate

▶ An officer shaking a fist in an inmate's face

TRUE/FALSE	**An inmate claiming mental cruelty can file a tort suit.**
	(18)
TRUE/FALSE	**Tort suits are filed in federal courts.**
	(22)

Tort Suits (continued)

A person who brings a tort action can win if he or she can show that the person sued caused some damage through being 1) negligent, 2) grossly negligent, or 3) willfully negligent. Legally, the alleged wrongdoer must have violated a duty owed to the person which, in turn, caused the injury or damage.

Let's take a closer look at the three types of negligence.

▶ **Negligence** is the failure to act as a *reasonable person* would in similar circumstances.

Example: While shutting a cell door behind an inmate, an officer doesn't look and accidentally shuts the door on the inmate's hand.

▶ **Gross Negligence** occurs when a person acts with reckless disregard for the probable consequences of his or her actions.

Example: A second officer likes to play a game to see how closely he can close the door behind the inmates. One day, he misses his mark and closes the door on an inmate's finger.

▶ **Willful negligence** occurs when a person intentionally engages in acts to cause harm.

Example: A third officer shuts the cell door on an inmate's hand on purpose.

In summary, when correctional staff breach or violate a duty owed to inmates and injure them, torts arise. The inmates may then file tort suits because of the injuries they received. If staff were negligent, grossly negligent or willfully negligent, they will be found liable.

Negligence is the failure to act as _____

_____ .

(26)

Willful negligence occurs when a person deliberately commits an act knowing that _____

_____ .

(30)

Gross negligence occurs when a person acts with _____

_____

for the probable consequences of his or her actions.

(34)

Civil Rights Actions

The majority of lawsuits filed by inmates against correctional staff are called civil rights actions. They are often referred to as "Section 1983" suits because the law that protects our civil rights is found under Section 1983 of Title 42 of the United States Code. Civil rights actions can be filed in state courts but are usually filed in federal courts.

These suits are popular for many reasons. Primarily, these actions have the potential to stop practices (e.g., discrimination) and to institute new ones. Moreover, they can be filed as "class action suits" for a "show of strength" and unity by inmates. If the actions succeed, the decisions benefit entire "classes" or groups of inmates instead of just the individual inmates who brought the suits.

Since 1976, under federal law, plaintiffs may receive money for injuries and for their attorneys' fees.

In corrections, common Section 1983 suits include:

▶ A complaint that inmate/attorney mail is being opened and read by correctional staff

▶ A complaint that a facility has inadequate living conditions

▶ A complaint that access to religious materials is being denied

---

TRUE/FALSE   Section 1983 suits can be filed as class action suits.

(2)

Civil rights actions can be used to _____ **practices or to** _____ **new ones.**

(5)

Civil Rights
Actions (continued)

To make a claim under Section 1983, a person must establish that another person, acting "under color of state law," caused a violation of a constitutional or federal statutory right. Let's break these criteria down.

▶ **Defendants must be "persons."** Civil rights actions can be brought only against "persons." Interestingly, the Supreme Court has ruled that cities and counties are "persons" and can be sued in a civil rights action. States are not "persons," however, and cannot be sued directly under Section 1983.

▶ **Defendants must be acting "under color of state law."** As a general rule, civil rights suits can be brought against government employees only for actions arising out of their employment—i.e, when they were acting "under color of state law."

▶ **The plaintiff must prove a violation of a constitutional or federal statutory right.** The action by the defendant must have caused a violation of a constitutional right (generally a right guaranteed by the U.S. Constitution) or a violation of a federal statutory right. Violations of federal statutes are rarely alleged in correctional lawsuits because very few federal statutes protect inmates.

In summary, when correctional staff violate inmates' constitutional rights, the inmates may file a civil rights action. Staff who have actually participated in, that is caused, the constitutional violation will be found liable.

The three criteria for establishing a Section 1983 case are:

- **The defendant must be a** _____.
  (10)

- **The defendant must be acting** _____.
  (16)

- **The plaintiff must prove a** _____
  of a constitutional or federal statutory _____.
  (21)

State Constitutional Rights Actions

More and more inmates are filing lawsuits that claim their *state* constitutional rights have been violated—because state constitutions often provide greater rights (that do not conflict with federal law) to inmates than the U.S. Constitution.

Sometimes state constitutional rights actions are filed directly in state courts. Or, sometimes these actions are added to Section 1983 lawsuits. This situation occurs when an inmate or group of inmates claim that staff and/or the facility violated both state and federal rights.

State constitutions often provide _____ rights than the U.S. Constitution.

(25)

Civil Cases—Potential Results

In a federal or state civil rights case, inmates may ask for:

▶ **Injunctive relief**—a court orders the facility or agency to perform a specific act or to stop performing such an act. For example, a court orders a facility to provide a legal library for inmate use.

▶ **Declaratory relief**—a court issues a judgment stating or "declaring" the rights of the inmates but does not order specific action or award damages. For example, a court declares that the conditions in an administrative segregation unit are so bad that they constitute cruel and unusual punishment. In some cases, the court will ask the facility or agency to submit a plan for remedying the conditions.

▶ **Money damages**—the court orders the institution or individual to pay a certain amount of money to the plaintiff.

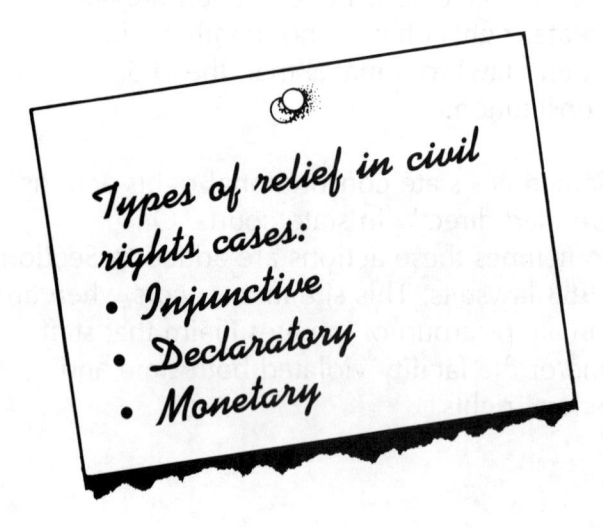

Types of relief in civil rights cases:
- *Injunctive*
- *Declaratory*
- *Monetary*

A court orders the warden of a facility to stop using inmates on road construction projects. This is an example of

_____ **relief.**
(28)

A court ruling states that sanitary conditions in a facility violate the inmates' constitutional rights. This is an example of _____ **relief.**
(33)

Money Damages

If the agency or staff are found liable in a civil rights suit *or* a tort suit, the inmate may receive nominal, compensatory or punitive damages.

▶ **Nominal damages**—will be awarded if the inmate's rights were violated, but he or she cannot show any actual harm. The amount will be "nominal," usually $1.00.

▶ **Compensatory damages**—will be awarded if the inmate proves the actual amount of damages sustained. The award is intended to compensate the inmate for the actual loss; it might be given for loss such as pain and suffering and mental anguish.

▶ **Punitive damages**—may be awarded to the inmate over and above the amount that would compensate for the loss. They are usually awarded only when staff knowingly violated the Constitution and/or acted in reckless disregard of the rights of the inmate. Punitive damages are intended to discipline the wrongdoer(s) and deter similar conduct by others in the future.

TRUE/FALSE In Section 1983 suits, inmates can receive only money for their injuries.
(36)

If an inmate can prove the actual amount of damages incurred, _____ will be awarded.
(39)

_____ are awarded when the actual amount of damages incurred is not proven.
(43)

If the defendant in a civil suit acted recklessly and maliciously, _____ can be awarded.
(47)

Good Faith

If the right allegedly violated in a civil rights case "was not clearly established," staff will be granted "qualified immunity"; consequently, they will not be required to pay damages. This situation is sometimes known as the "good faith" defense. It protects only employees—it does not protect a government agency if that agency, such as a city or county, is otherwise subject to damages.

Despite the implications from the name "good faith defense," an employee's good intentions or good faith are of little relevance in establishing a good faith defense. The defense does not focus on the employee's state of mind. Rather, it focuses entirely on the state of the law at the time of the incident: was or was not the right "clearly established."

As correctional law continues to evolve and develop, more and more rights are becoming "clearly established." Therefore, potential liability for damages is increasing.

The key factor in determining a good faith defense is whether the right _____ at the time of the incident.
(3)

TRUE/FALSE   A good faith defense protects only state governments.
(7)

Tort Actions vs. Civil Rights Actions

Often, the legal burden (what an inmate must prove) differs between a tort action or a civil rights action—even though the facts of the case are the same. For example, suppose an inmate feels she has received inadequate medical care. In a tort case, she would need to prove that the alleged wrongdoer was negligent. In a civil rights case, however, she would need to prove that the alleged wrongdoer was "deliberately indifferent to her medical needs." Deliberate indifference often is a more difficult burden than negligence.

Still, even when the burden is greater, inmates prefer to file civil rights actions for three reasons:

1) Historically, federal courts (where civil rights cases are usually brought) have been seen as more sympathetic to inmate claims than state courts (where tort suits are filed).

2) Inmates may get broader relief in a civil rights case. No injunctive relief is available in a tort action. Moreover, some states limit the amount of damages that can be awarded against staff or immunize staff from damages altogether. Finally, some states do not allow punitive damages.

3) Attorneys' fee awards are available in civil rights cases but not tort suits. Recent Supreme Court decisions have placed restrictions on the size of fee awards but their mere existence is appealing to inmates.

Inmates prefer to file civil rights cases because:

- _____ courts have been seen as more sympathetic to inmate claims than _____ courts.
  (11)

- These cases offer _____ relief.
  (14)

- _____ are available.
  (17)

CHAPTER 2: CIVIL LIABILITY IN CORRECTIONS

Supervisory Liability—Section 1983 Cases

A person is liable under Section 1983 when he or she "causes one to be subject to" a constitutional violation. Courts are now frequently asked to focus on this phrase to assess potential liability on the part of supervisors—who did not directly participate in the challenged act or omission. These cases often focus on one of two specific areas:

1) **Failure to Supervise.** Suppose a supervisor may have, or reasonably should have, knowledge of a pattern of constitutionally offensive acts but fails to take corrective action. The supervisor may be liable if his or her actions were "deliberately indifferent" to the constitutional rights of the victim. An example of "failure to supervise" might be where a supervisor is aware of staff using excessive force against inmates but does nothing to correct the situation.

2) **Failure to Train.** Suppose an officer is not properly trained in an area. If the failure to train is so serious to be considered "deliberately indifferent" to the constitutional rights of an inmate, the supervisor may be held liable. This situation might occur if a supervisor assigns a new officer to a "constitutionally sensitive" position—knowing that the officer did not have training in the constitutional issues involved.

For instance, suppose an officer does not understand that inmates may have a constitutionally protected right to use the library as part of their right of access to the courts. His supervisor assigns him to the facility law library, knowing full well about the officer's lack of training in this area. One day, the officer decides that an inmate has been "wasting too much time in the library lately" and refuses to let him use it. The supervisor could be potentially liable even though he or she was not directly involved in the actions of the officer.

Supervisory liability in Section 1983 cases hinges on whether the supervisors were _____ to the inmates' constitutional rights.

(20)

Supervisory Liability— Section 1983 Cases (continued)

There are other supervisory failures that can potentially lead to supervisory liability under Section 1983. These include such things as improper supervision or assignment, gross failure in retention (retaining a clearly incompetent staff member) and failure in direction of staff.

The common link in all of these areas is: where the supervisor's alleged failure can be tied directly to the actual violation, and it can be said that but for the failure of the supervisor, this violation probably would not have occurred. In this sense, the courts will say the supervisor "caused" the violation.

Most lawsuits about improper training or supervision are not brought against the trainer or first level supervisor. Instead, the inmate sues the agency or agency head, claiming the inadequate training or supervision reflected agency policy or custom.

Check the situations that can expose a supervisor to liability in a civil rights action.

_____ A. Supervising an officer improperly

_____ B. Retaining a clearly incompetent officer

_____ C. Failing to see that an officer is properly trained

_____ D. Failing to direct an officer properly

_____ E. Assigning an officer improperly

(24)

Supervisory Liability (continued)

People can be held responsible for the actions of others under a concept called *vicarious liability*. When applied to the employer-employee relationship, it is called *"respondeat superior,"* which means "let the superior answer."

In corrections, a supervisor may be held responsible for and, therefore liable, for the torts or wrongful acts that employees commit during the scope of employment. To be held liable, the supervisor must have failed to direct or train an officer, or must have been negligent in hiring, supervising, assigning or retaining an officer.

To prove negligence on the part of the supervisor, an inmate must show that the supervisor knew or should have known of the officer's past negligent conduct or habits.

Once again, the inmate is more likely to sue the agency or the agency head, rather than the supervisor.

"Respondeat superior" — let the superior answer.

TRUE/FALSE The standard for supervisory liability in tort suits is deliberate indifference.
(27)

TRUE/FALSE Inmates are more likely to sue an agency head than a supervisor.
(32)

Review of the Law

Let us review what we have covered thus far:

▶ Our law is divided into two categories: criminal law and civil law.

▶ In criminal cases, people are accused of committing crimes against the public—even though there may be only one victim. State or federal government representatives, therefore, prosecute the accused.

▶ Civil law pertains to the private rights of individuals and the legal proceedings connected with these rights.

▶ The three common types of civil lawsuits brought by inmates against correctional staff are:

— Tort suits—an inmate claims that he or she has suffered an injury because of the fault of one or more staff members.

— Civil rights actions—an inmate (or inmates) alleges that one or more staff and/or the facility have violated his or her constitutional rights.

— State constitutional rights actions—an inmate (or inmates) alleges that one or more staff and/or the facility have violated his or her *state* constitutional rights.

▶ A person who brings a tort action can win if he or she can show that the person sued caused some damage through being:

— Negligent—the failure to act as a *reasonable person* would in similar circumstances.

— Grossly negligent—the person acts with reckless disregard for the probable consequences of his or her actions.

— Willfully negligent—the person intentionally engages in acts to cause harm.

▶ The types of damages in a civil rights suit or a tort suit are:

— Nominal damages—will be awarded if the inmate's rights were violated, but he or she cannot show any actual harm.

— Compensatory damages—will be awarded if the inmate proves the actual amount of damages sustained.

— Punitive damages—may be awarded to the inmate over and above the amount that would compensate him or her for the loss.

▶ Two specific areas of supervisory liability in Section 1983 cases are:

— Failure to supervise

— Failure to train

Inmates' Rights

As you have learned, many of the lawsuits brought by inmates allege that correctional officers have violated their rights. You should not spend time, worrying, however, about whether *your staff* will make costly mistakes. Instead, you should be proactive. In other words, be familiar with inmates' rights so that you can properly assess your staff's interaction with inmates and take steps to avoid liability. One expert summarized this approach well: "don't let loose cannon balls roll around on your deck."

In the next section of this chapter, we will review the basic rights of inmates in these key areas:

▶ Searches

▶ Use of force

▶ Medical and mental health care

▶ Conditions of confinement

▶ Access to the legal system

▶ Religion, speech and press

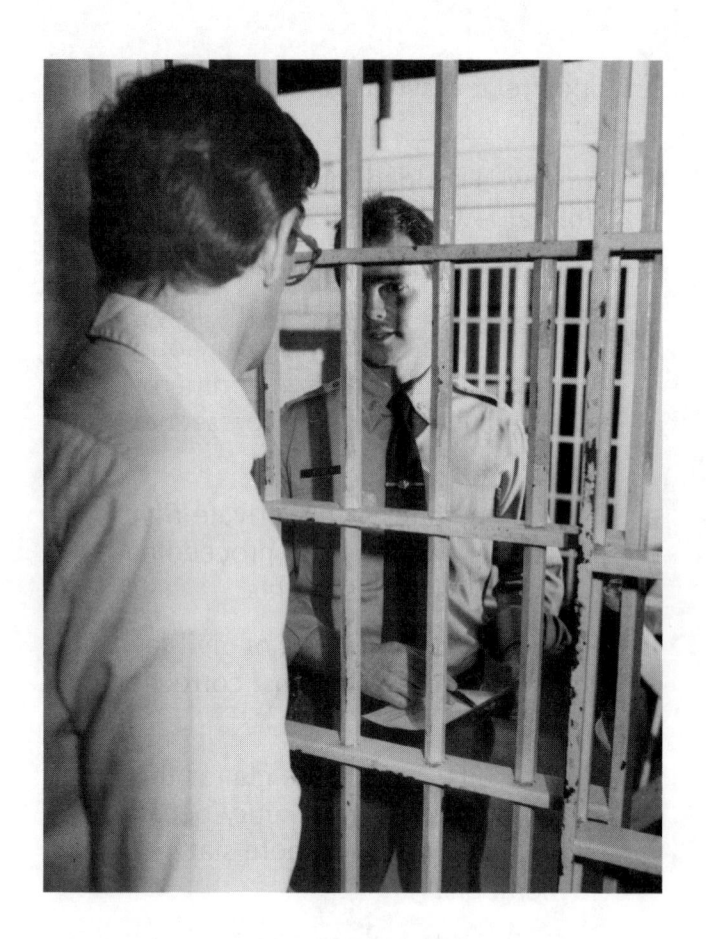

Inmates' Rights— Searches

The Fourth Amendment to the U.S. Constitution guards against unreasonable searches of persons and their property. It reads:

> The right of people to be secure . . . against unreasonable searches and seizures shall not be violated without probable cause.

In the correctional environment, searches are necessary to ensure the security of the institution and the safety of inmates and staff. Both inmates and pre-trial detainees have the right to be free from unreasonable searches and seizures. The question then becomes, "What is a reasonable search?"

To answer this question, we will address each type of search on the next several pages.

The Fourth Amendment to the U.S. Constitution protects citizens against _____ searches and seizures.

(29)

Searches are necessary for correctional facilities to maintain _____ and _____ .

(37)

TRUE/FALSE The Fourth Amendment *does not* apply to pre-trial detainees.

(41)

CHAPTER 2: CIVIL LIABILITY IN CORRECTIONS III—85

Inmates' Rights— Cell or Property Searches

The first type of search we will examine is the cell or property search. The Supreme Court has said that cells may be searched randomly, routinely and without warrants. The inmate does not have to be present during the search, but officers should treat the inmate's belongings with appropriate respect.

The Court has not decided yet whether inmates are entitled to receipts for contraband seized during cell or area searches. However, most institutional regulations require receipts as a good management practice. Some also require a second officer to be present when items are removed to witness what occurs.

In general, pre-trial detainees must submit to a search of any personal property that they wish to take into or out of the institution. But such searches are only to be used to make sure that contraband neither enters nor leaves the institution.

Note: The same guideline applies to staff and visitors.

Cell searches may be conducted randomly, routinely and without warrants.

Place a check beside each statement that is true.

_____ A. An inmate must be present when his or her cell is searched.

_____ B. Convicted inmates and pre-trial detainees are treated the same in regard to cell or property searches.

_____ C. Cells may be searched randomly and routinely.

_____ D. A warrant must be obtained for a cell search.

(45)

Inmates' Rights— Pat/Frisk Searches

Pat down searches of inmates may be conducted on a routine basis without a warrant for any legitimate security concern. Moreover, pre-trial detainees may be patted down upon arrest and booking.

NOTE: Pat down searches of correctional staff may be performed only when there is a strong reason to believe that they are concealing dangerous contraband. Visitors should be patted down only when there is a strong reason to believe that they possess contraband which threatens security. Such searches are only permitted when visitors are told they may be searched upon entering the facility grounds.

Which of these groups may be subjected to a pat or frisk search on a routine, random basis?

_____ A. Pre-trial detainees

_____ B. Staff

_____ C. Inmates

_____ D. Visitors

(49)

Inmates' Rights—
Strip Searches

According to the Supreme Court, inmates may be strip searched after they come into contact with the general public. A strip search should be conducted in a reasonable manner and provide as much privacy as possible. It should be done by members of the same sex as the inmate, if possible. If not, the circumstances should be thoroughly documented.

Many experts believe that routine strip searches of inmates cannot be conducted without "a reasonable belief" or "a real suspicion" that contraband is concealed on the person.

Lower courts have consistently ruled that *routine* strip searches of pre-trial detainees are not acceptable. There may be some circumstances, however, under which a pre-trial detainee must be strip searched. Check with your legal counsel to verify when such searches might be appropriate—for inmates as well as staff and visitors.

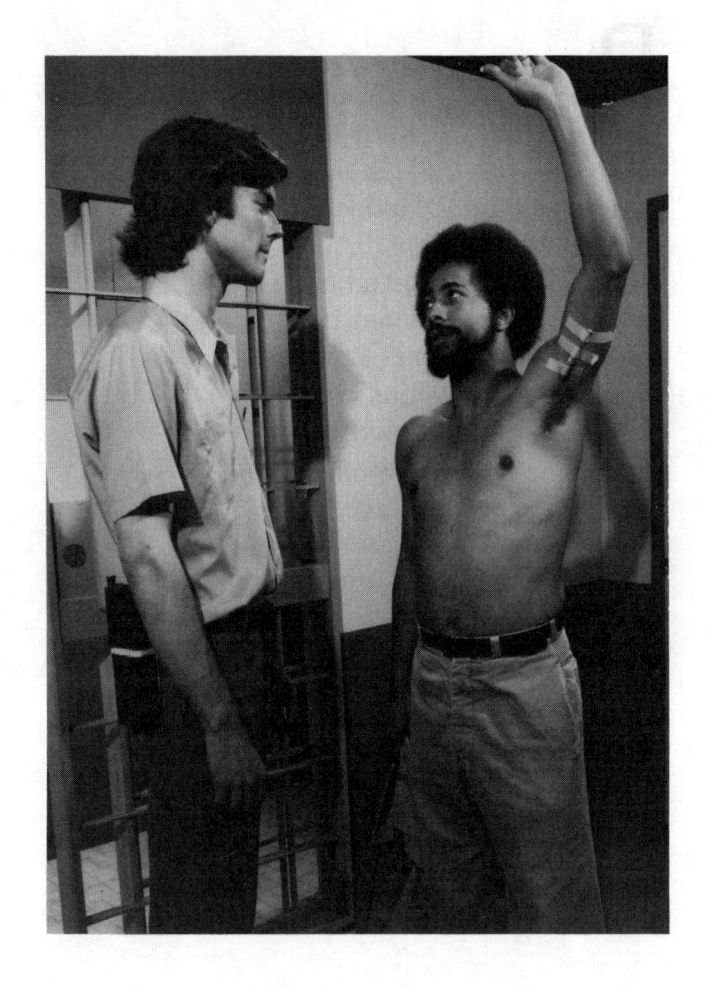

TRUE/FALSE   Inmates may be strip searched on a routine basis.

(51)

Strip searches should be conducted in a _____ manner and provide as much _____ as possible.

(54)

TRUE/FALSE   Pre-trial detainees may be strip searched on a routine basis.

(57)

Inmates' Rights— Body Cavity Searches

Body cavity searches should be conducted only when there is a "clear indication" that the inmate is hiding contraband in a body cavity. They require written approval of the warden or superintendent or someone he or she designates. Upon approval, the searches should be conducted by medical personnel only.

RANDOM URINALYSIS AND AIDS TESTING

Random urinalysis and AIDS testing are considered to be a search. You should verify your institution's policy on these issues.

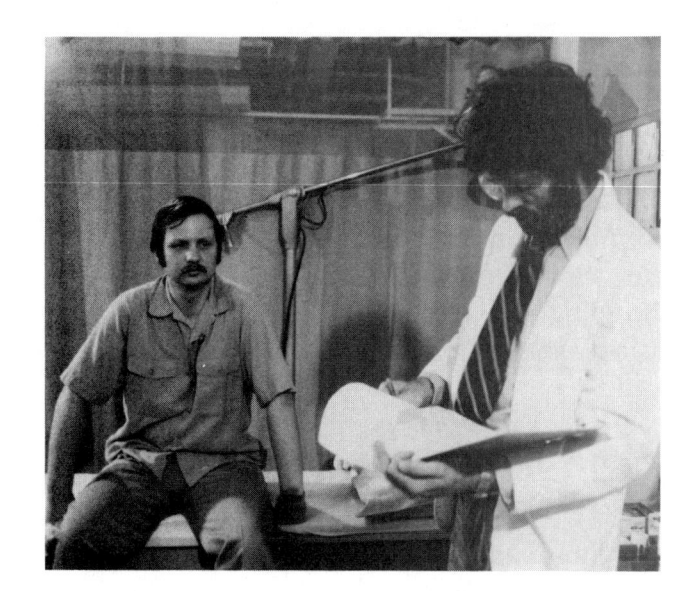

Match the following.
1. Cell or property searches
2. Pat/frisk searches
3. Strip searches
4. Body cavity searches

_____ A. Can be conducted on inmates on a random, routine basis

_____ B. Require written approval from the warden or superintendent

_____ C. Inmates may be subjected to this search after contact with the general public

_____ D. Should be conducted only by medical personnel

(31)

Inmates' Rights— Use of Force

In certain situations, correctional personnel have the right and the duty to use force. The use of force can be defined as *the unwanted touching of one person by another*. This may involve direct physical contact or the putting into motion of an object that touches the individual. So, for example, throwing an object at an inmate, or using a water cannon against rioters *are* uses of force.

The use of force can be divided into two categories—*non-deadly* and *deadly*.

▶ **Non-deadly force** does not cause death or serious injury.

▶ **Deadly force** might cause death.

The number of incidents involving non-deadly force far out-weigh those involving deadly force.

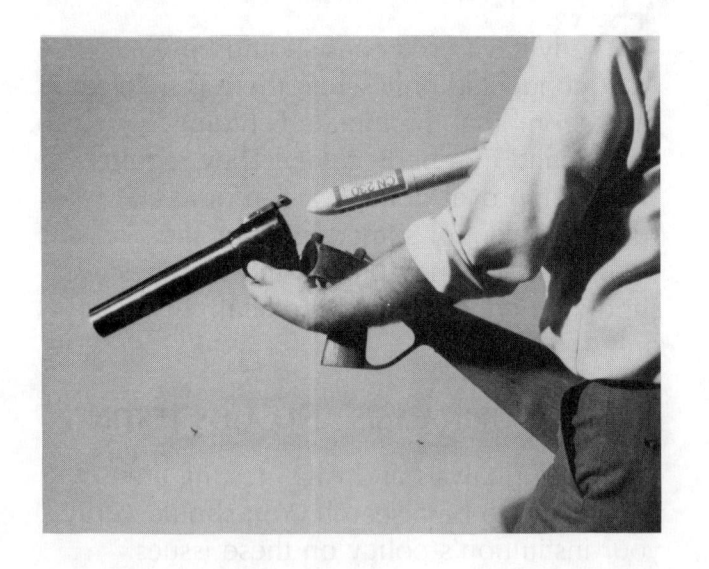

Which *is not* a use of force?

_____ A. Hitting an inmate with a riot baton

_____ B. Spraying mace on an inmate

_____ C. Yelling at an inmate

_____ D. Restraining an inmate

(35)

The use of force is _____

_____.

(38)

Inmates' Rights—
Use of Force (continued)

The law requires that the use of force be *reasonable* and *necessary*. This means that force must not exceed the amount necessary to get the job done.

To determine *reasonableness*, the courts examine the circumstances of the event in question. They consider several factors, including:

▶ The amount of force correctional personnel are responding to—the force shown by the inmate

▶ The reasonable perception of danger

▶ The existence of non-forceful alternatives

▶ The size and strength of the officer versus the inmate

▶ The inmate's history of violence

To determine whether reasonable force is *necessary*, courts use legally recognized bases. These include:

▶ In self-defense and in the defense of others

▶ To prevent a crime (including escape)

▶ To detain or arrest an inmate

▶ To preserve order and maintain security

What does reasonable and necessary force mean?

_____

_____

(40)

List two factors in determining whether force is *necessary*.

• _____

• _____

(44)

List two factors used in determining whether force is *reasonable*.

• _____

• _____

(48)

Inmates' Rights— Use of Deadly Force

The U.S. Supreme Court ruled that deadly force should be used only as a last resort:

▶ To prevent serious bodily harm or death

▶ To prevent the commission of a felony (including escape)

At any other time, the use of deadly force may result in civil and/or criminal liability against the correctional officer, his or her supervisor, the agency or the agency head.

When can deadly force be used?

- _____
- _____

(52)

Inmates' Rights—The Use of Chemical Agents and Mechanical Restraints

Chemical agents and mechanical restraints should be used only when reasonably necessary.

Chemical agents should be used only by officers trained in their use. They should not be used without proper approval, and they should not be used repeatedly against the same inmate within a short period of time.

Correctional experts disagree about which causes more harm—chemical agents or physical force. Inmates may have allergic reactions to the chemicals. Inmates also might be harmed if they are not allowed to wash a chemical agent off their skin shortly after its use. Many courts believe that chemical agents represent a greater amount of force than physical force.

Mechanical restraints may be used to transport inmates or to restrain inmates—when officers suspect, from the inmates' behavior, that the inmates will injure themselves or others.

No type of force may be used to punish inmates or to intentionally cause them discomfort or pain.

Force cannot be used to _____ inmates or to intentionally cause them _____.

(56)

Inmates' Rights—
Medical and Mental Health Care

Correctional facilities are responsible for providing for the well-being of their inmate populations. This means that correctional facilities must provide the health care that inmates receive—either directly (by administering it) or indirectly (by bringing it in). *Correctional staff may not prevent access to this care.*

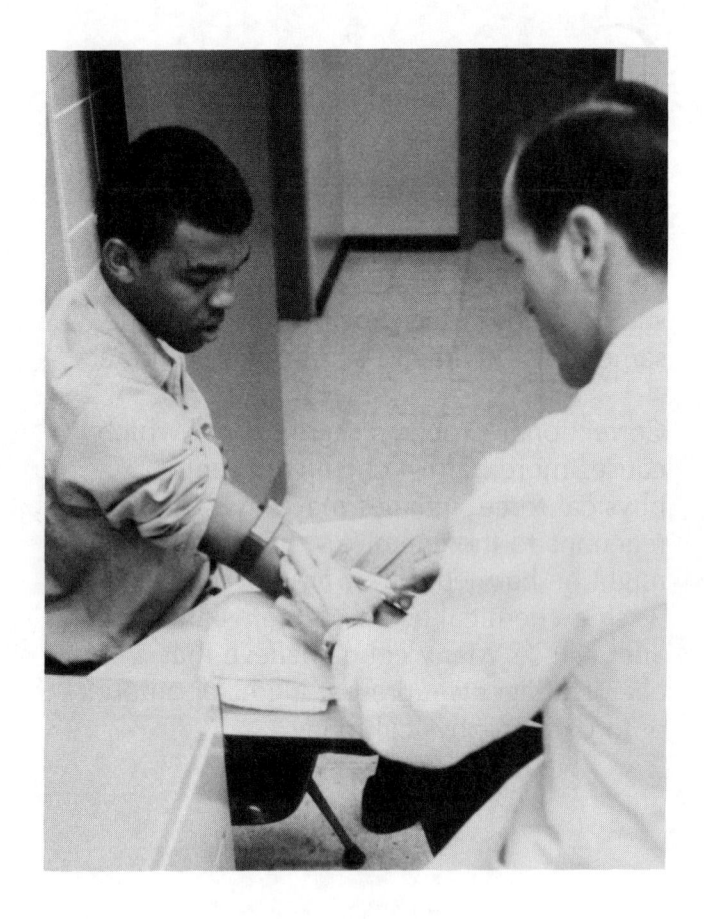

In fact, they can be held liable if they are found to be "deliberately indifferent" to an inmate's serious medical needs.

"Deliberate indifference" occurs when:

▶ No response to a serious medical need is given

▶ The response to a serious medical need is inadequate

In addition, correctional staff can be held liable if they were negligent in responding to an inmate's medical needs.

Inmates' Rights—Medical and Mental Health Care (continued)

TRUE/FALSE The U.S. Constitution guarantees inmates specific standards of medical care.

(59)

TRUE/FALSE Staff can make minor medical decisions—for example, whether an inmate really needs to see medical staff in the middle of the night.

(62)

Officer Kane collects the "sick call slips" and accidentally loses Inmate Donner's slip on the way to the medical unit. Inmate Donner, a diabetic, is later rushed to the hospital because of major complications. Was Officer Kane negligent? Why?

_____
_____
_____
_____

(65)

An inmate complains of serious stomach pains for weeks on end. Officer Brown gives him over-the-counter antacids but refuses to let him see the doctor. The inmate loses consciousness as the result of a massive stomach ulcer. Is this deliberate indifference to serious medical needs? Why?

_____
_____
_____
_____
_____

(69)

Inmates' Rights—Suicide Prevention

Correctional facilities and staff are not no-fault insurers of inmates who attempt suicide. But correctional staff do have a duty to protect inmates from themselves. Therefore, staff cannot simply brush off potential suicide liability by saying that "we can't be responsible for what someone does to himself."

As a supervisor, you can help prevent suicides and potential liability by ensuring that your staff:

▶ **Identify potential suicidal inmates.** Be sure that your staff know the verbal and non-verbal signs and symptoms of suicidal behavior.

▶ **Make appropriate referrals.** Verify that your staff know how to refer potentially suicidal offenders to mental health staff.

▶ **Communicate to other staff about potentially suicidal offenders.** Reiterate to your staff that they must keep other staff informed of any current information about potentially suicidal offenders.

▶ **Communicate with suicidal offenders.** Confirm that your staff know the proper ways to communicate with suicidal inmates.

▶ **Monitor suicidal inmates properly.** Go over these important guidelines with your staff: You should *not* place potentially suicidal offenders in isolation unless you can *constantly* supervise them. If you cannot constantly supervise these inmates, then place them with two or more other offenders. These "cellmates" can serve as companions—not staff—and call for help if an emergency arises. Under these conditions, you need to supervise the potentially suicidal offenders *at least every 10 minutes*. If you place potentially suicidal offenders in suicide-resistant rooms, you need to supervise them every *three to four minutes*.
Note: Two-thirds of suicides occur in isolation.

▶ **Respond promptly and appropriately to suicide attempts.** Check to make sure that your staff know how to respond to a suicide attempt. For example, staff should know the method of quickly cutting down a hanging victim, plus other immediate first-aid measures.

▶ **Document attempted or completed suicides.** Be sure that your staff know how to report and document attempted or completed suicides.

List two ways that a supervisor can prevent liability in suicide-related lawsuits.

• _____

• _____

(42)

Correctional staff have a _____

_____ **inmates from themselves.**

(46)

Inmates' Rights— Conditions of Confinement

Inmates have the right to live in an environment that is safe, sanitary and humane. Protecting this right is a challenge in many crowded facilities. Staff cannot use crowding, however, as an excuse to neglect their responsibilities toward inmates. To do so would "invite" lawsuits and expose staff to liability.

You cannot control crowding in your facility, but you *can* have an impact upon the conditions of confinement. And, you can take steps to avoid liability. Here are some suggestions for two key areas: sanitation and safety.

SANITATION

Make sure that your staff insist on clean and sanitary work areas. Instruct your officers to require inmates to clean up after themselves and to keep common/living areas clean and orderly. These practices will go a long way toward creating acceptable living conditions.

SAFETY

The law does not guarantee inmates' safety. But you and your staff have a duty to protect inmates from one another and to maintain generally acceptable levels of safety. Therefore, be sure that your staff are following facility policies and procedures relating to safety. To make a quick evaluation, ask yourself questions such as: Are the inmates reasonably safe—or is there an inmate who is at serious risk of assault, rape or other serious injury from another inmate? Are the staff properly trained in areas relating to safety—spotting signs of trouble, using communication skills to calm an inmate and so forth? Do staff respond properly to requests for protective custody? medical attention?

List two things you can do to have a positive impact on the conditions of confinement.

- _____
- _____

(50)

Inmates' Rights—Segregation

Inmates placed in disciplinary or administrative segregation may have limited access to certain programs of the institution due to custody level or segregation status. But, like other inmates, inmates in segregation are entitled to receive the essentials for survival, including food, water, and the basics for sanitation.

And, these inmates are entitled to:

- ▶ Adequate access to the courts—although the legal access provided to segregated inmates can be *different* from that provided to other inmates.

- ▶ Adequate access to religious materials and/or counseling—inmates who are in administrative or disciplinary segregation may be prevented from attending *group* religious services, but they cannot be denied the right to practice their religion; they also cannot be denied counseling.

Segregated inmates . . . entitled to adequate access to the courts and religious materials.

Inmates in segregation cannot be denied:

- _____
- _____
- _____
- _____

(53)

Inmates' Rights— Access to the Legal System

Correctional facilities are responsible for providing inmates with the legal access they are due. Let's take a look at their specific rights in this area.

PRIVILEGED COMMUNICATION

Correctional staff have a duty to ensure the privacy of written and spoken communication between inmates and their lawyers. Specifically, the courts have said that:

▶ Lawyers must be allowed free access to their clients unless the requested visiting time is clearly unreasonable.

▶ Lawyer/client interviews are protected from being listened to by correctional personnel. However, for security purposes, they can be monitored visually.

▶ Incoming mail from attorneys can be inspected for contraband, but it may not be read by correctional personnel.

▶ Outgoing mail to attorneys cannot be opened or read.

▶ Correctional staff have the right to make sure that a visiting person is actually a legal practitioner.

Privileged communication... written and spoken communication between inmates and their lawyers.

TRUE/FALSE	Inmates may not be denied the right to have contact visits with their attorneys. (55)
TRUE/FALSE	Inmates are entitled to the same privacy whether they're talking to their lawyers or to visitors. (60)
TRUE/FALSE	Correctional staff can search and read mail that is coming from or going to an attorney. (64)

Inmates' Rights—
Access to the Legal System (continued)

"JAILHOUSE LAYWERS"

Correctional facilities must allow "jailhouse lawyers" to provide legal advice or assistance if there is no other competent legal advisor available. On the other hand, the courts have recognized that correctional staff may place some restrictions on "jailhouse lawyers" in the interest of order and security. Here are some general rules:

▶ "Jailhouse lawyers" may not be punished for helping other inmates with legal matters or for expressing their opinions. On the other hand, they are not immune from normal disciplinary procedures; "jailhouse lawyers" who violate the normal rules of conduct at a facility can be disciplined just like other inmates.

▶ Inmates cannot be denied access to "jailhouse lawyers." The activities of "jailhouse lawyers," however, can be restricted as to time and place.

▶ Correctional facilities have the right to make sure that no payment (e.g., money, contraband or favors) is given to "jailhouse lawyers" for their services; most correctional facilities forbid any bartering arrangements between inmates. Officers who become aware of any payment arrangements have the right to prevent them from being carried out—and the duty to report the arrangements to their supervisors.

Place a "T" by the statements that are true, an "F" by the statements that are false.

_____ A. Correctional staff can restrict where and when "jailhouse lawyers" help fellow inmates.

_____ B. "Jailhouse lawyers" are entitled to be paid for their services, like other legal advisors.

_____ C. "Jailhouse lawyers" are not immune from disciplinary procedures.

_____ D. Inmates can be denied access to "jailhouse lawyers" at the discretion of correctional staff.

(68)

Inmates' Rights—
Freedom of Religion, Speech and Press

The First Amendment to the U.S. Constitution says,

> Congress shall make no law respecting the establishment of religion, or prohibiting the free exercise thereof; or abridging the freedom of speech, or the press. . . .

Inmates *do* have the fundamental right to freedom of speech, religion and press. But facilities may limit these rights—so long as the regulations are reasonably related to the genuine interests of the facilities.

If the regulations also affect others outside the facility (for example, publishers who want inmates to read their publications), then the facilities also must *prove* that their regulations are *necessary*.

TRUE/FALSE Correctional facilities cannot limit inmates' right to freedom of religion, speech and press.

(72)

Inmates' Rights— Freedom of Religion

While inmates' right to *believe* is absolute, their right to practice a religion in a correctional facility is not so sweeping. Some restrictions can be justified on the basis of institutional security and order. The courts generally recognize that inmates have the right to:

▶ Assemble for religious purposes

▶ Receive and read religious material

▶ Wear certain religious emblems

▶ Consult and correspond with the clergy for religious purposes

While these rights extend to members of traditional religious groups (such as Catholics, Protestants and Jews), they also extend to other, less traditional, groups. For instance, courts have recently held that witchcraft and Rastafarianism (a Jamaican system of beliefs) are legitimate religions.

The right to practice other religious observances, such as having access to "sweatboxes," is less clear because meeting the requests of one group may impose a hardship on other inmates, institutional staff or facility resources. Facilities can restrict these practices if administrators can demonstrate that there is an immediate need to do so—based on a recognized institutional goal, such as to preserve order and maintain security.

Religious restrictions can be justified.

Restrictions on inmates' freedom of religion can be justified only because of legitimate institutional goals like _____ **and** _____.

(58)

List two religious rights of inmates.

• _____

• _____

(63)

TRUE/FALSE Inmates' religious rights extend only to members of traditional groups.

(67)

III–102   CHAPTER 2: CIVIL LIABILITY IN CORRECTIONS

Inmates' Rights— Freedom of Speech

In general, inmates can believe whatever they wish, and express those beliefs freely. Inmates cannot be punished for merely saying what they truly believe. If inmates urge others to *act*, however, then the facility can restrict their freedom of speech. The same holds true if the facility believes the inmate's speech will endanger the security of the institution.

The freedom of speech provision of the First Amendment also protects the rights of inmates to correspond with others outside the institution. Correspondence can be by mail, telephone and visitation. But, once again, the right is not absolute.

An inmate's mail may be opened and inspected for contraband. Correctional officers can refuse to deliver the contents if it clearly threatens the security of the institution (escape plans, coded messages and so forth).

Inmates should be provided ample opportunities for visitation and for contacting their families and others by telephone. Facilities can place restrictions on these privileges but courts require administrators to prove that such restrictions are necessary.

TRUE/FALSE The Constitution guarantees inmates complete freedom of speech.

(61)

For what reason may correctional officers refuse to deliver inmates' mail?

_____

_____

(70)

TRUE/FALSE Correctional facilities cannot place restrictions on inmates' visits and contacts with family members.

(73)

Inmates' Rights—
Freedom of the Press

The courts have held that the public's right to publish and distribute material should be protected more vigorously than inmates' rights to the same freedoms. Let's take a look at what rights inmates retain in this area.

The Right to Publish Materials for Distribution Within the Facility

Many correctional facilities allow their inmates to publish newsletters for distribution within the facility. From time to time, correctional facilities have censored the contents of these newsletters to preserve order and maintain security. Such censorship generally has been upheld by the courts.

Under what circumstance may correctional administrators decide to censor inmate publications?

_____
_____
_____

(75)

TRUE/FALSE The courts have held that, when it comes to freedom of the press, inmates' rights are more limited than the general public's.

(78)

Inmates' Rights—
Freedom of the Press (continued)

The Right to Receive Printed Matter

This right is more protected than inmates' right to publish and distribute their own printed matter. In fact, facilities must have a compelling reason to censor incoming materials. But, once again, printed materials are not immune from searches for contraband. Moreover, the *amount* of printed materials within a cell can be limited due to health or safety concerns, such as fire.

TRUE/FALSE The amount of printed material an inmate keeps in his cell cannot be limited by correctional authorities.

(82)

Inmates' right to _____

is more protected than their right to

_____.

(85)

Inmates' Rights— Review

In this section of the chapter, you learned the following things.

▶ Inmates are protected by the Fourth Amendment to the U.S. Constitution against unreasonable searches.

- Cell or property and pat down or frisk searches can be conducted randomly on a routine basis for any legitimate security concern
- Inmates can be strip searched after they come in contact with the general public
- Pre-trial detainees cannot be routinely strip searched
- Body cavity searches can be conducted only when there is a "clear indication" that the inmate is hiding contraband
- Body cavity searches should be conducted by medical personnel only

▶ Use of force is the unwanted touching of one person by another. The two classes of force are:

— Non-deadly—does not kill or cause serious injury

— Deadly—force that might cause death

▶ Considerations in determining whether the use of force was justified are:

— Reasonableness:

- The amount of force correctional personnel are responding to—the force shown by the inmate
- The reasonable perception of danger
- The existence of non-forceful alternatives
- The size and strength of the officer versus the inmate
- The inmate's history of violence

— Necessity

- In self-defense and in the defense of others
- To prevent a crime
- To detain or arrest an individual inmate
- To preserve order and maintain security

▶ Deadly force can be used only as a last resort

- To prevent serious bodily harm or death
- To prevent the commission of a felony (including escape)

▶ No type of force may be used to punish inmates or to intentionally cause them discomfort or pain.

Inmates' Rights—
Review (continued)

- Correctional staff cannot prevent inmates from having access to medical and mental health care.

- Deliberate indifference in medical and mental health occurs when:
    - An essential component of the health care delivery system is missing
    - No response to a serious medical need is given
    - The response to a serious medical need is inadequate

- Correctional staff have a duty to protect inmates from themselves.

- Correctional administrators and all staff have a responsibility to maintain their facilities in a safe, sanitary and humane condition.

- Correctional facilities are responsible for providing inmates with the legal access they are due.

- Correctional staff have a duty to ensure the privacy of written and spoken communication between inmates and their lawyers

- Correctional facilities must allow "jailhouse lawyers" to provide legal advice or assistance if there is no other competent legal advisor available

- Inmates in disciplinary or administrative segregation are entitled to receive the essentials for survival, adequate access to the courts, and adequate access to religious materials and counseling.

- Inmates are to be given the same basic rights as all citizens in regard to freedom of religion, speech and the press as long as these rights do not conflict with the correctional concerns of order and security.

Legal Representation and Indemnification

Thus far in this chapter, you have learned some basics about the law and reviewed many of the basic rights that are the common subjects of lawsuits.

This section of the chapter addresses two concerns that correctional staff have about being sued: legal representation and indemnification (reimbursement for any damages assessed against them).

Legal representation: The agency may provide an attorney to defend a correctional employee in a lawsuit.

Indemnification: The agency may pay for damages assessed against a correctional employee in a civil suit—if the employee was acting within the policies and procedures of the institution.

TRUE/FALSE Your agency will pay for any damages assessed against you in a civil suit.

(66)

Legal Representation and Indemnification (continued)

LEGAL REPRESENTATION

Most states or institutions will defend their employees in *civil* suits. This defense is provided only if the employees have acted within the scope of their employment—within the guidelines of their job descriptions and within the established policies of their facility.

For *local* employees, legal representation varies from facility to facility. Some local institutions use county or district attorneys to represent their employees, while others allow the officers to choose a lawyer who is then paid by the institution.

For *state* employees, representation also varies. Often, the attorney general will be asked to serve as legal representative for state employees. Where this practice is not possible, states will permit the hiring of outside lawyers to defend their employees—at the state's expense. In some cases, if the action causing the lawsuit is covered by an insurance policy, the insurer's attorney most likely will represent the officer.

The Federal Bureau of Prisons provides *federal* officers with legal representation, either through regional offices or through the central office.

Legal representation for corrections employees varies from facility to facility.

Most states and local agencies will defend their employees in civil suits as long as they have acted within the _____. (71)

Legal Representation and Indemnification (continued)

CRIMINAL SUITS

Criminal suits present a different picture for correctional employees. Many agencies will not defend a staff member who is charged in a criminal suit. In fact, the state is often the prosecutor against its own staff member in these situations.

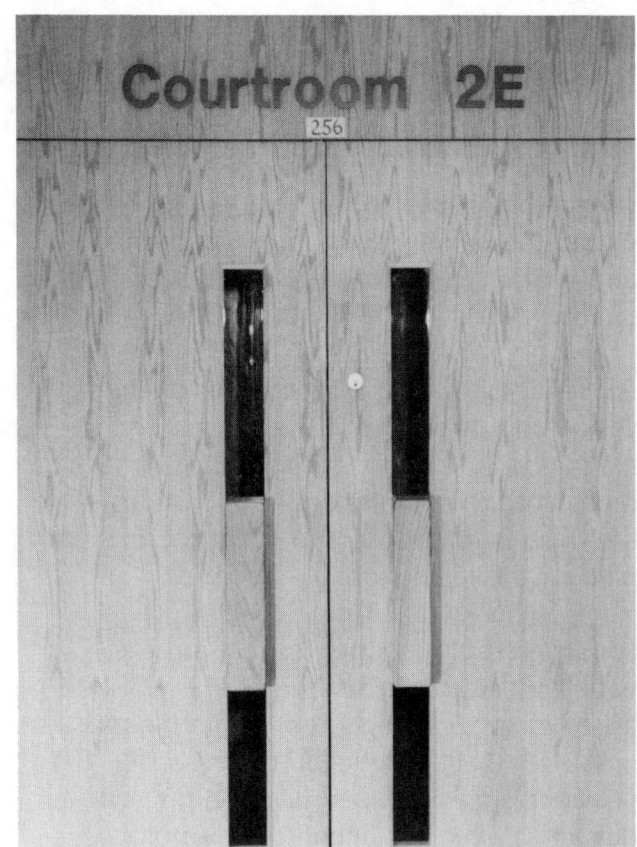

In which of these cases would an agency probably provide legal representation?

_____ A. Officer Jan Lincoln is accused of bringing drugs into an institution.

_____ B. Inmate Duggan is suing because Officer Williams took away Duggan's crutches for security reasons.

_____ C. Officer Genton is charged with driving a government vehicle while under the influence.

_____ D. Inmate Coleman's family is claiming that Officer Lowell failed to monitor the suicidal inmate properly.

(74)

Legal Representation and Indemnification (continued)

INDEMNIFICATION

Among the first concerns correctional employees have about lawsuits are, "Will I have to pay damages? Will I have to pay for my attorney?" The answer to these questions is generally "No."

State Employees

Virtually every state in the country has a procedure by which state employees sued in the line of work are indemnified for any costs of litigation—including attorneys' fees and damages. Even when a judgment is against the defendant "personally," the state typically pays the judgment.

In general, the state is not under a duty to provide legal representation and indemnification if the actions of the employee were outside the scope of the employee's duties or were not taken in good faith.

Employees of Local Governments

It is a little more difficult to generalize about the protections employees of local governments enjoy in this area. Some localities may provide protection similar to that enjoyed by state employees. Other jurisdictions may carry insurance or self-insure.

Both state and local government employees should determine the scope of protection they have for legal representation and indemnification.

What does indemnification mean?

_____
_____
_____
_____

(76)

When can the state refuse to provide legal representation and indemnification?

• _____
• _____

(81)

Legal Representation and Indemnification (continued)

INSURANCE

Some states and local jurisdictions have purchased insurance to cover correctional staff for potential liability awards. Several have laws that both authorize and require such insurance.

In states or jurisdictions where legal representation or indemnification is uncertain, personal insurance might be a good idea. But it is expensive and may provide only limited coverage. Before purchasing such insurance, therefore, you should consult your institution's attorney—to get his or her analysis of the personal risks involved and the kind and amount of protection the insurance offers. If an attorney is not available, you should consult your superior.

Consult your institution's attorney regarding liability insurance.

TRUE/FALSE All states have liability insurance for correctional staff.

(84)

Legal Representation and Indemnification (continued)

For your own protection and knowledge, you should ask your superiors and legal advisors about representation and indemnification. Questions that should be asked include:

▶ If I am sued in a criminal, tort, or civil rights action in a state or federal court, will my agency provide a lawyer to represent me?

▶ Does our state have laws that would indemnify me if I am found liable in a state or federal civil rights action or in a tort case? How do these laws apply to me?

▶ Is there any kind of liability insurance available to me through the government or private companies?

Preventing Liability

Now that you have completed sections on the law, inmates' rights and representation and indemnification, you are ready to apply all the principles you learned to prevent liability.

There are several steps that you can take to prevent liability. Following these steps won't prevent lawsuits, but they should help you and your staff avoid being held liable.

1. Follow written and verbal instructions carefully; keep current.

2. Seek clarification for any policy, procedure or instruction that you don't fully understand.

3. Review policies, procedures and post orders regularly.

4. Be sure that your subordinates know what is expected of them and that they understand policies, procedures and post orders.

5. Maintain good records and make sure that your staff do likewise.

6. Review your subordinates' reports.

7. Take prompt corrective action if a policy or procedure isn't followed by a member of your staff.

Each of these steps will be examined on the following pages.

Preventing Liability (continued)

1. FOLLOW WRITTEN AND VERBAL INSTRUCTIONS CAREFULLY; KEEP CURRENT

If you follow your agency's written and verbal instructions, you will be in the best possible position to avoid liability. Remember at all times that how you carry out policies and procedures will influence your staff. Therefore:

▶ **Follow established policies and procedures in your daily activities.** Your staff will mirror your actions; therefore, if you ignore or shortcut policies and procedures, they will do the same.

▶ **Be positive about reasons for "doing it by the book."** As a member of the management team, you must occasionally "sell" your staff on the reasons for a new procedure or technique.

▶ **Monitor your staff.** Properly monitoring or supervising your staff is critical to preventing liability.

In addition to following instructions carefully, you need to keep current on any changes in your facility's policies and procedures—and any new court rulings, trends in corrections and so forth.

"Do it by the book."

Your staff will _____ your actions.

(88)

Preventing Liability (continued)

2. SEEK CLARIFICATION FOR ANY POLICY, PROCEDURE OR INSTRUCTION THAT YOU DON'T FULLY UNDERSTAND

In Chapter 1 of Book I, you learned that you are both a supervisor *and* a subordinate. You both receive and give orders and directives. If you don't understand a policy, procedure or instruction, you can't properly present it to your staff. Therefore, if you do not understand a directive or instruction, ask your superior about it. Many times, questions will clarify the area of uncertainty.

TRUE/FALSE If you're unclear about a policy, you will not be able to present it properly to your staff.

(91)

Preventing Liability (continued)

3. REVIEW POLICIES, PROCEDURES AND POST ORDERS REGULARLY

Special circumstances may require your staff to do things that aren't part of normal daily operations. A fire, an escape attempt, an inmate in a diabetic coma, and a visitor refusing to be searched are examples of such special circumstances. By reviewing policies, procedures and post orders periodically, you'll know how to train your staff so that they will be able to react appropriately when these situations arise.

A good way to do this is to review a policy or procedure as a regular part of your staff meeting. Take one a week—for example, part of your roll-call can be devoted to a particular rule. This way, every policy and procedure will be reviewed.

TRUE/FALSE Policies and procedures should be made a regular part of any staff meeting.

(77)

Preventing Liability (continued)

4. BE SURE THAT YOUR SUBORDINATES UNDERSTAND WHAT IS EXPECTED OF THEM AND THAT THEY UNDERSTAND POLICIES, PROCEDURES AND POST ORDERS

As a supervisor, you are responsible for the actions of your staff. Therefore, you must carefully evaluate:

▶ Post assignments—can the person handle the job you assigned?

▶ Directions—have you properly alerted staff to potential problems? Were you clear in your orders? Did you get feedback that your staff understood their responsibilities?

▶ On-the-job training experiences—did the staff member learn the proper procedure?

Three ways to prevent liability are:

- Follow written and verbal instructions
  _____

- When in doubt, ask _____

- Review policies, procedures and post orders
  _____

(79)

TRUE/FALSE Making sure that your subordinates know the **rules, procedures and post orders** is as important as knowing them yourself.

(83)

III–118   CHAPTER 2: CIVIL LIABILITY IN CORRECTIONS

Preventing Liability (continued)

5. MAINTAIN GOOD RECORDS

Having the documentation to prove that your instructions and procedures were properly followed is a strong defense against personal liability. Items such as your critical incident log (covered in Chapter 3 of Book II) will provide written historical information and can be used to support an officer's actions, as well as your decisions.

6. REVIEW SUBORDINATES' REPORTS

Any time one of your staff writes a report of any kind, you should review it. For example, any incident between a staff member and an inmate that gets "written-up" needs your attention. This is especially true if there was an improper interpretation of a policy or procedure by a staff member. Reports are often the official account of an incident. Should there be a hearing or trial, the report will be an important piece of evidence. Therefore, your review should include making sure that the report was done properly and accurately.

TRUE/FALSE   Maintaining good records is important for accreditation purposes only.
(87)

TRUE/FALSE   You should review the reports of your staff only when they contain an unusual occurrence.
(89)

Preventing Liability (continued)

7. TAKE PROMPT CORRECTIVE ACTION IF A POLICY OR PROCEDURE ISN'T FOLLOWED

This is one area where many supervisors have some difficulty. It is important to make sure that you consistently take prompt action when there is a violation of a policy or procedure. There should be no exceptions. If a procedure, policy or post order applies to the newest member of your staff, then it applies to the most senior veteran. Everyone must work by the same set of rules. If they don't, then it is you, the supervisor, who may be held liable.

Occasionally, you may have to take disciplinary action against a member of your staff for failing to follow policies and procedures. Areas of action that require your immediate intervention are:

▶ Misuse of equipment

▶ Mistreatment of inmates

▶ Staff who are reckless or incompetent

▶ Ethical violations

As a supervisor, you must _____ take corrective action when a policy or procedure isn't followed.
(80)

To prevent personal liability, you should:

- **Be sure your staff both know and** _____ the rules, procedures and post orders.
(86)

- **Maintain good** _____
(92)

- _____ your subordinate's reports.
(90)

- **Take** _____ **corrective action** when a policy or procedure isn't followed.
(93)

Preventing Liability (continued)

The guidelines you just learned about should help you prevent liability, both for you and your staff. You should:

▶ Follow written and verbal instructions carefully; keep current

▶ Seek clarification from your superior

▶ Regularly review policies, procedures and past orders for your benefit and that of your staff

▶ Train your staff in policies and procedures

▶ Keep good records and make sure that your staff do likewise

▶ Review your staff's reports

▶ Take corrective action immediately when necessary

If you make a conscious effort to follow these guidelines, you should feel secure that you—and your staff—will be free from the risk of liability.

You can help prevent liability for yourself and your staff.

Summary

Let's summarize the main points in this chapter.

▶ The three types of civil lawsuits that inmates file are:

- Tort suits—Claim that one party has suffered some sort of injury because of the fault of another party. They usually seek monetary damages.

- Civil rights actions—Allege that one party (usually the government) has violated the constitutional rights of another party and seek an end to such violations.

- State constitutional rights actions—Similar to civil rights actions except they allege violation of the *state constitution,* rather than the U.S. Constitution.

▶ The three degrees of fault in a tort action are:

- Negligence—the failure to act as a reasonable person would in similar circumstances.

- Gross negligence—when a person acts with reckless disregard for the probable consequences of his or her actions.

- Willful negligence—when a person intentionally engages in an act to cause harm.

▶ The three forms of relief in civil rights actions are:

- Injunctive relief—a court orders someone to perform a specific act or to stop performing such an act.

- Declaratory relief—a court issues a judgment stating or "declaring" the rights of the parties but does not order specific action or award damages.

- Money damages—the court orders the institution or individual to pay a certain amount of money to the inmate.

▶ The three types of damages one may receive in a civil suit are:

- Nominal damages—may be awarded when the inmate fails to prove the actual amount of damages incurred.

- Compensatory damages—will be awarded if the inmate proves the actual amount of damages sustained.

- Punitive damages—may be awarded to the inmate over and above what will compensate for the loss, if the defendant acted in a wanton, reckless, malicious or fraudulent manner.

Summary (continued)

- Inmates are protected by the Fourth Amendment to the U.S. Constitution against unreasonable searches.
  - Cell or property and pat down or frisk searches can be conducted randomly on a routine basis for any legitimate security concern
  - Inmates can be strip searched after they come in contact with the general public
  - Pre-trial detainees cannot be routinely strip searched
  - Body cavity searches can be conducted only when there is a "clear indication" that the inmate is hiding contraband
  - Body cavity searches should be conducted by medical personnel only
- Use of force is the unwanted touching of one person by another. The two classes of force are:
  - Non-deadly—does not kill or cause serious injury.
  - Deadly—force that might cause death.
- Considerations in determining whether the use of force was justified are:
  - Reasonableness:
    - The amount of force correctional personnel are responding to—the force shown by the inmate
    - The reasonable perception of danger
    - The existence of non-forceful alternatives
    - The size and strength of the officer versus the inmate
    - The inmate's history of violence
  - Necessity
    - In self-defense and in the defense of others
    - To prevent a crime
    - To detain or arrest an individual inmate
    - To preserve order and maintain security
- Deadly force can be used only as a last resort
  - To prevent serious bodily harm or death
  - To prevent the commission of a felony (including escape)
- No type of force may be used to punish inmates or to intentionally cause them discomfort or pain.
- Correctional staff cannot prevent inmates from having access to medical and mental health care.

Summary (continued)

- Deliberate indifference in medical and mental health occurs when:
  - An essential component of the health care delivery system is missing
  - No response to a serious medical need is given
  - The response to a serious medical need is inadequate
- Correctional staff have a duty to protect inmates from themselves.
- Correctional administrators and all staff have a responsibility to maintain their facilities in a safe, sanitary and humane condition.
- Correctional facilities are responsible for providing inmates with the legal access they are due.
  - Correctional staff have a duty to ensure the privacy of written and spoken communication between inmates and their lawyers
  - Correctional facilities must allow "jailhouse lawyers" to provide legal advice or assistance if there is no other competent legal advisor available
- Inmates in disciplinary or administrative segregation are entitled to receive the essentials for survival, adequate access to the courts, and adequate access to religious materials and counseling.
- Inmates are to be given the same basic rights as all citizens in regard to freedom of religion, speech and the press as long as these rights do not conflict with the correctional concerns of order and security.
- Most states or institutions will defend their employees in *civil* suits—if the employees have acted within the scope of their employment.
- Indemnification is the process whereby an agency may pay for damages assessed against a correctional employee in a civil suit.
- The principles that will help you prevent personal liability are:
  - Follow written and verbal instructions; keep current.
  - Seek clarification for any policy, procedure or instruction that you don't fully understand.
  - Review policies, procedures and post orders regularly.
  - Be sure that your staff know what is expected of them and that they understand policies, procedures and post orders.
  - Maintain good records and make sure that your staff do likewise.
  - Review your subordinates' reports.
  - Take prompt corrective action if a policy or procedure isn't followed by a member of your staff.

Answer Key—Civil Liability in Corrections

1. Match the following.

    1. Plaintiff
    2. Defendant
    3. Civil law
    4. Criminal law

    __1__ A. The "victim" of wrongful actions

    __2__ B. The person accused of a wrongful action(s)

    __3__ C. Cases decided on the basis of a preponderance of the evidence

    __1__ D. The government fulfills this role in criminal cases

2. **True.** Section 1983 suits are used as a "show of strength" and unity by inmates.

3. The key factor in determining a good faith defense is whether the right **was clearly established** at the time of the incident.

4. Match the following.

    1. Civil case
    2. Criminal case

    __1__ A. Sex discrimination

    __2__ B. Assault

    __2__ C. Bank robbery

    __2__ D. Drug trafficking

    __1__ E. Slander

    __1__ F. Cruel and unusual punishment

    __1__ G. Freedom of religion

    __1__ H. Sexual harassment

5. Civil rights actions can be used to **stop** practices or to **institute or start** new ones.

6. **True.** Both inmates and staff have rights that are protected by the courts. Many of the staff rights were explained in Chapter 1 of this book. You will learn more about inmate rights in this chapter.

Answer Key—Civil Liability in Corrections (continued)

7. **False.** A good faith defense protects only *employees*.

8. An inmate claiming a violation of her First Amendment right of free speech would file a **civil rights** suit.

9. The number of lawsuits in the United States is **increasing.**

10. The defendant in a Section 1983 case must be a **person.**

11. Inmates prefer to file civil rights cases because **federal** courts have been seen as more sympathetic to inmate claims than **state** courts.

12. Two ways that you can reduce your fear about lawsuits are:
    - Be aware of the concerns that the courts have singled out
    - Know your agency's policies and procedures

13. An inmate claiming a staff member caused his leg injury would file a **tort** suit.

14. Inmates prefer to file civil rights cases because these cases offer **broader** relief.

15. **True.** Because criminal cases are crimes against the public, state or federal government representatives prosecute the accused.

16. The defendant in a Section 1983 case must be acting **under the color of state law.**

17. Inmates prefer to file civil rights cases because **attorneys' fee awards** are available.

18. **True.** An inmate claiming mental cruelty can file a tort suit.

19. Victims in criminal cases **do not** receive compensation for their injuries.

20. Supervisory liability in Section 1983 cases hinges on whether the supervisors were **deliberately indifferent** to the inmates' constitutional rights.

Answer Key—Civil Liability in Corrections (continued)

21. The plaintiff in a Section 1983 case must prove a **violation** of a constitutional or federal statutory **right.**

22. **False.** Tort suits are filed in state courts.

23. **True.** The prosecutor is the representative of the government. The victims rely on the prosecutor to represent their interests.

24. The situations that can expose a supervisor to liability in a civil rights action include:

    √ A. Supervising an officer improperly

    √ B. Retaining a clearly incompetent officer

    √ C. Failing to see that an officer is properly trained

    √ D. Failing to direct an officer properly

    √ E. Assigning an officer improperly

25. State constitutions often provide **greater** rights than the U.S. Constitution.

26. Negligence is the failure to act as **a reasonable person would in similar circumstances.**

27. **True.** The deliberate indifference implies that the supervisor failed to train or direct an officer or was negligent in supervising, assigning or retraining an officer.

28. A court orders the warden of a facility to stop using inmates on road construction projects. This is an example of **injunctive** relief.

29. The Fourth Amendment to the U.S. Constitution protects citizens against **unreasonable** searches and seizures.

30. Willful negligence occurs when a person deliberately commits an act knowing that **harm will likely result.**

Answer Key—Civil Liability in Corrections (continued)

31. Match the following.

    1. Cell or property searches
    2. Pat/frisk searches
    3. Strip searches
    4. Body cavity searches

    __1,2__ A. Can be conducted on inmates on a random, routine basis

    __4__ B. Require written approval from the warden or superintendent

    __3__ C. Inmates may be subjected to this search after contact with the general public

    __4__ D. Should be conducted only by medical personnel

32. **True.**

33. A court ruling states that sanitary conditions in a facility violate the inmates' constitutional rights. This is an example of **declaratory** relief.

34. Gross negligence occurs when a person acts with **reckless disregard** for the probable consequences of his or her actions.

35. The action below which **is not** a use of force is:

    _____ A. Hitting an inmate with a riot baton

    _____ B. Spraying mace on an inmate

    __✓__ C. Yelling at an inmate

    _____ D. Restraining an inmate

36. **False.** Inmates may ask for injunctive relief, declaratory relief or monetary damages.

37. Searches are necessary for correctional facilities to maintain **security** and **safety.**

38. The use of force is **the unwanted touching of one person by another.**

Answer Key—Civil Liability in Corrections (continued)

39. If an inmate can prove the actual amount of damages incurred, **compensatory damages** will be awarded.

40. Reasonable and necessary force means that **the force must not exceed the amount necessary to get the job done.**

41. **False.** The Fourth Amendment applies to both convicted inmates and pre-trial detainees.

42. The ways a supervisor can prevent liability in suicide-related lawsuits are to make sure that staff:
    - Identify potential suicidal inmates
    - Monitor suicidal inmates properly
    - Make appropriate referrals
    - Communicate to other staff about potentially suicidal offenders
    - Communicate with suicidal offenders
    - Respond promptly and appropriately to suicide attempts
    - Document attempted or completed suicides properly

43. **Nominal damages** are awarded when the actual amount of damages incurred is not proven.

44. Factors in determining whether force is necessary include:
    - In self-defense and in the defense of others
    - To prevent a crime (including escape)
    - To detain or arrest an inmate
    - To preserve order and maintain security

Answer Key—Civil Liability in Corrections (continued)

45. The true statements are:
    - _____ A. An inmate must be present when his or her cell is searched.
    - __✓__ B. Convicted inmates and pre-trial detainees are treated the same in regard to cell or property searches.
    - __✓__ C. Cells may be searched randomly and routinely.
    - _____ D. A warrant must be obtained for a cell search.

46. Correctional staff have a **duty to protect** inmates from themselves.

47. If the defendant in a civil suit acted recklessly and maliciously, **punitive damages** can be awarded.

48. Factors used in determining whether force is reasonable include:
    - The amount of force correctional personnel are responding to—the force shown by the inmate
    - The reasonable perception of danger
    - The existence of non-forceful alternatives
    - The size and strength of the officer versus the inmate
    - The inmate's history of violence

49. The group that may be subjected to a pat or frisk search on a routine, random basis is:
    - _____ A. Pre-trial detainees
    - _____ B. Staff
    - __✓__ C. Inmates
    - _____ D. Visitors

50. Two things you can do to have a positive impact on the conditions of confinement are:
    - Emphasize sanitation
    - Make safety a priority

Answer Key—Civil Liability in Corrections (continued)

51. **False.** Unlike pat searches, strip searches should be conducted when there is a "reasonable belief" or "real suspicion" that contraband is concealed.

52. The two conditions in which deadly force may be used are:
    - To prevent serious bodily harm or death
    - To prevent the commission of a felony (including escape)

53. Inmates in segregation cannot be denied:
    - Essentials for survival
    - Access to courts
    - Access to religious materials
    - Access to counseling

54.. Strip searches should be conducted in a **reasonable** manner and provide as much **privacy** as possible.

55. **True.** Inmates must be able to communicate with their attorneys.

56. Force cannot be used to **punish** inmates or to intentionally cause them **discomfort or pain.**

57. **False.** Courts have ruled that pre-trial detainees may **not** be strip searched on a routine basis.

58. Restrictions on inmates' freedom of religion can be justified only because of a legitimate institutional goal like **preserving order** and **maintaining security.**

59. **False.** The courts do not guarantee inmates specific standards of medical care.

60. **False.** Inmates are entitled to *more* privacy when they're talking to their lawyers.

Answer Key—Civil Liability in Corrections (continued)

61. **False.** The correctional system *can* impose some restrictions on an inmate's freedom of speech.

62. **False.** Correctional staff are not trained to make medical diagnoses.

63. In the area of religion, inmates have the right to:
    - Assemble for religious purposes
    - Receive and read religious material
    - Wear certain religious emblems
    - Consult and correspond with the clergy for religious purposes

64. **False.** They may search the mail for contraband, but they cannot read it.

65. Yes, Officer Kane could be found negligent. There was no intent to deny medical treatment. The officer lost the request; he did not ignore it. However, there may be some liability even if the loss was accidental.

66. **False.** The agency *may* pay for damages assessed, depending on the circumstances of your action.

67. **False.** Less traditional religious groups have the same rights as those who practice traditional religions.

68. "T" marks the statements that are true; "F" marks the statements that are false.

    - __T__ A. Correctional staff can restrict where and when "jailhouse lawyers" help fellow inmates.
    - __F__ B. "Jailhouse lawyers" are entitled to be paid for their services, like other legal advisors.
    - __T__ C. "Jailhouse lawyer" are not immune from disciplinary procedures.
    - __F__ D. Inmates can be denied access to "jailhouse lawyers" at the discretion of correctional staff.

69. Yes, this is a case of deliberate indifference to medical needs. Staff may not prevent access to medical care.

Answer Key—Civil Liability in Corrections (continued)

70. Correctional officers may refuse to deliver inmates' mail if the contents threaten the security of the institution.

71. Most states and local agencies will defend their employees in civil suits as long as they acted within the **scope of their employment.**

72. **False.** Correctional facilities may limit inmates' rights to freedom of religion, speech and the press as long as the limits are reasonably related to the interests of the facilities.

73. **False.** The restrictions must be *necessary.*

74. An agency probably would provide legal representation in these cases:

    ____ A. Officer Jan Lincoln is accused of bringing drugs into an institution.

    √ B. Inmate Duggan is suing because Officer Williams took away Duggan's crutches for security reasons.

    ____ C. Officer Genton is charged with driving a government vehicle while under the influence.

    √ D. Inmate Coleman's family is claiming that Officer Lowell failed to monitor the suicidal inmate properly.

75. Correctional administrators may censor inmate publications when they pose a threat to order or security.

76. Indemnification means **the agency pays or reimburses the employee for civil damages.**

77. **True.** Anytime your staff gets together, there is an opportunity to review policies and procedures.

78. **True.** The courts have held that the public's right to publish and distribute material should be protected *more* vigorously than inmates' rights to do so.

79. Three ways to prevent liability are:

    - Follow written and verbal instructions **carefully**
    - When in doubt, ask **questions**
    - Review policies, procedures and post orders **regularly**

Answer Key—Civil Liability in Corrections (continued)

80. As a supervisor, you must **consistently** take corrective action when a policy or procedure isn't followed.

81. The state can refuse to provide legal representation and indemnification when:
    - The employee acted outside the scope of employment
    - The employee's action was not in good faith

82. **False.** The amount of printed material in an inmate's cell *can* be limited for health and safety reasons.

83. **True.** Remember, as a supervisor, you get work done through others.

84. **False.** You should talk with your superior about what's available in your state.

85. Inmates' right to **receive printed materials** is more protected than their right to **publish and distribute materials.**

86. To prevent personal liability, you should be sure that your staff both know and **understand** the rules, procedures and post orders.

87. **False.** Maintaining good records is important for many aspects of your job.

88. Your staff will **mirror** your actions.

89. **False.** You should review *all* the reports written by your staff.

90. To prevent personal liability, you should **review** your subordinate's reports.

91. **True.** You are in a position to get clarification from your captain, lieutenant or warden.

92. To prevent personal liability, you should maintain good **records.**

93. To prevent personal liability, you should take **prompt** corrective action when a policy or procedure isn't followed.

CHAPTER 3

The Disciplinary Process

Objectives

At the end of this chapter, you will be able to:

▶ Explain why policies and work rules are necessary.

▶ List the two reasons why enforcement of policies and procedures is necessary.

▶ List the five areas of supervisory responsibility in disciplining staff.

▶ Differentiate between major and minor offenses.

▶ List the five factors that supervisors must consider when setting the penalty for a minor offense.

Introduction

Throughout this course you have learned several factors for effective correctional supervision. Among these were:

▶ Supervisors get their work done through others.

▶ An employee represents a major investment by the agency.

▶ Through an effective orientation and training program, a supervisor sets the tone for working with a new employee.

▶ Interpersonal communication skills are critical in daily relationships with staff.

▶ Agency rules and regulations must be known, taught and enforced.

▶ Performance evaluations and coaching sessions are critical to continued good performance as well as improvement where there may be deficiencies.

Despite your best efforts, you must be prepared for the eventuality that some staff will break work rules or fail to follow the procedures of your agency. In most cases, when this happens, you will attempt to improve performance through the use of IPC skills, coaching and training. If these efforts fail, you will need to initiate disciplinary procedures.

This chapter deals with the purposes of discipline, the concept of corrective discipline and disciplinary procedures. Throughout the chapter, discipline will be defined as a way to correct behavior—not punish it.

TRUE/FALSE Some staff inevitably will fail to follow agency procedures or will break work rules.

(7)

TRUE/FALSE Any disciplinary procedure should be viewed as the first step in trying to improve staff performance.

(12)

The Disciplinary Process

The steps that are followed in the disciplinary process are basically the same in all correctional facilities. Every agency, though, has its own specific policies and procedures, which can be found in the policies and procedures manual. The steps detailed below, therefore, are generally true for all facilities. But you should check your agency's manual for the specific procedures to be followed in your facility.

1. You have determined that a violation of one of the work rules has occurred. You know that this work rule has been enforced consistently through the years. You already have tried improving this employee's performance through performance evaluations and coaching. You decide, therefore, that you must discipline this subordinate.

2. You conduct an investigation of the incident, gathering all the facts that you can.

3. You determine the appropriate charge for the violation. The possible charges are listed in the policy manual.

4. You determine the appropriate penalty for this charge. The range of penalties is listed in the policy manual.

5. The Disciplinary Review Committee (or similar group) holds a hearing. This committee is usually made up of a union representative, someone from the Personnel Department, your superior and yourself. In some instances, the charged employee and his or her witnesses have the opportunity to present evidence. This Committee confirms that a thorough investigation has been conducted, and then decides whether the charge and the penalty are appropriate.

6. If the Disciplinary Review Committee confirms your charge and penalty, then the employee is subject to the penalty specified.

7. If the Disciplinary Review Committee finds your charge and penalty to be in error, then it can recommend one of the following:

— A new investigation be conducted

— The charge be dropped

— A lesser or greater penalty be imposed

The steps that you must take will be discussed in more detail throughout this chapter.

Purposes of Discipline

In general, policies and work rules are necessary to:

▶ Ensure that the agency meets its goals or mission

▶ Have a standardized staff response to a given situation

▶ Protect the welfare of both staff and inmates

Usually, about 95% of an agency's disciplinary problems come from about 5% of its employees. This means that the overwhelming majority of employees will willingly obey policies and work rules most of the time.

However, you cannot simply hope that your staff will fall into the larger group. As a supervisor, you are responsible for enforcing policies and work rules in your unit. Thus, you must take action when any employee fails to follow a policy or breaks a work rule.

TRUE/FALSE Most employees will require some form of disciplinary action.

(18)

List two reasons why work rules and policies are necessary.

• _____

• _____

(22)

CHAPTER 3: THE DISCIPLINARY PROCESS   III–139

Purposes of Discipline (continued)

Enforcing work rules or maintaining discipline is an important part of your job for three reasons. First, the rules have been established for good reason. If they are continually violated, the efficiency and effectiveness of the agency will be compromised as will the safety of staff and inmates.

Second, most employees want to work in an orderly and safe environment. They look to their supervisor—you—to meet this need. If you overlook violations by one or more employees, the environment may become— or have the perception of becoming— disorderly and potentially unsafe. Consequently, the staff (including the ones who break the rules) will lose respect for you, believing that you are weak. In addition, the morale of those who are willingly obeying the rules will deteriorate.

Finally, "inadequate supervision" can lead to lawsuits and potential liability. One area that falls under the heading of "inadequate supervision" is the failure to enforce work rules and agency policies. If you don't maintain discipline in your unit by enforcing the rules, you may be guilty of "inadequate supervision." The ensuing lawsuit may result in liability not only for you but also for your superiors. In some cases, even the agency head or agency itself may be found liable.

One way to maintain discipline is by

_____.

(1)

The continued violation of rules could eventually jeopardize the _____ of staff and inmates.

(5)

Experience shows that when a supervisor deliberately overlooks work violations by an employee:

TRUE/FALSE   The morale of rule-abiding employees decreases.

(8)

TRUE/FALSE   The employee who broke the rules will eventually stop.

(11)

TRUE/FALSE   The supervisor will lose the respect of his or her employees.

(15)

The Supervisor's Responsibility

Most supervisors understand the importance of enforcing work rules and policies. But, like many of your colleagues, you may be concerned about how your performance in this area will be evaluated by your superior. And, you may be concerned about how your staff will react. You want to discipline them to maintain order, yet you also want to earn their respect to develop workable relationships.

The basis of your evaluation will be whether you acted responsibly. If you can answer "Yes" to each of the questions below, you will know that you are on solid ground. You will know that you have done a good job of enforcing work rules and policies, of maintaining discipline. You also will know that you have most likely earned the respect of your staff because you have acted fairly in maintaining order in the unit.

▶ Was the policy or work rule clearly communicated?

▶ Has the rule or policy been consistently enforced?

▶ Was the investigation thorough and unbiased?

▶ Is the level of evidence or proof adequate?

▶ Was the penalty proper in view of all relevant considerations?

We will discuss each of the issues raised above in the following pages.

Communication

In employee relations, ignorance *is* an excuse. If an employee does not know a particular work rule, he or she has a valid excuse for not obeying that rule. As a supervisor, therefore, you must make a conscientious effort to communicate all policies and work rules to each member of your staff. If you do not make this effort, you will lose your ability to enforce policies and rules.

The best time to start making sure that policies and rules are well-known is during orientation and training. Discuss one-on-one with all new hires the "way things are done" and why. Also explain what happens when an employee violates a policy or breaks a rule; present the consequences as the agency's and not yours. Be sure to hold such discussions again whenever changes occur to major policies and rules.

Remember, however, that even though new hires are your major concern, you must communicate the same information to **everyone** you supervise.

For this reason, some agencies take additional steps in communicating policies and work rules. For example, an agency might post them on a bulletin board, and distribute them in an employee handbook and/or policies and procedures manual.

TRUE/FALSE An employee who does not know a particular work rule has a valid excuse for not obeying that rule.

(20)

List at least two ways to communicate policies and work rules to employees.

- _____
- _____

(25)

Consistent Enforcement

Some supervisors want to be "good-guys"; others want to avoid a conflict or a hassle. Consequently, they fall into the trap of believing that occasional violations of a policy or work rule will not cause a problem. The truth, however, is that a problem may occur if a supervisor fails to enforce a policy or work rule over a period of time. Thus, as a supervisor, you must be concerned with consistent enforcement.

Consistency is also important for three other reasons. As we mentioned earlier, inconsistent enforcement within your group can have disastrous effects. The environment may be—or have the perception of being—disorderly and potentially unsafe. Hence, all the staff, including the violator, lose respect for you. And, the morale of the staff who follow the rules declines.

Inconsistency also can have a poor effect beyond a particular unit. Suppose, for example, that you do not enforce a certain rule. An employee in the group then transfers to another unit where the supervisor takes the opposite approach. The employee quickly gets "into hot water" for breaking the rule. He does not understand what has happened, and why his new boss is concerned. Meanwhile, the other employees probably are trying to figure out why the "new guy" nonchalantly ignored the rule. After all, they have never broken it. This awkward situation could have been avoided if all the supervisors in your facility were consistently enforcing policies and rules.

Consistent Enforcement (continued)

Finally, inconsistent enforcement over a period of time can lead to liability for improper supervision. A court may conclude that the agency's "real policy/rule is to do what employees actually do, not what the policies and procedures manual says to do." This concept is known as a binding "past precedent." It means that because you didn't enforce a policy or procedure in the past, you can't expect it to be followed in the present.

In other words, if you don't use your "enforcement authority" over a period of time, you lose it—even though the policy or procedure may be written in your agency's manual. Moreover, when a new supervisor comes in, he or she can't immediately enforce the policy because a precedent was set.

For a precedent to become binding, there must have been frequent violations and there must be clear evidence that you, the supervisor, knew about the violations but did nothing about them. If only a single violation occurred or if you were unaware of the violations, the precedent does not become binding.

Inconsistent enforcement ... can lead to liability.

Failing to consistently enforce a policy or work rule may establish a _____.
(2)

TRUE/FALSE Ignoring just one single violation is enough to establish a precedent.
(6)

Consistent Enforcement (continued)

CASE STUDY

The written policy of Midview Correctional Facility states that staff may not deposit inmate mail in a local post office or mail box.

Officer Glenn Gibbs has been approached often by inmates to deposit letters for them—emergency situations, children's birthdays, letters to attorneys. He and several other officers will do this favor if the inmate has been straight with them in the past. Glenn's supervisor knows this act is a violation of policy, but officers were depositing inmate mail long before he became supervisor. In fact, he did it when he was an officer.

A letter threatening to kill a judge was sent from an inmate at Midview. The subsequent investigation revealed that Officer Gibbs mailed the letter for the inmate—in violation of institution policy.

Should past precedent apply in any disciplinary action taken against Officer Gibbs?

_____ Yes   _____ No

Because: _____

_____

_____

_____

(13)

Consistent Enforcement (continued)

If a precedent becomes binding, you—or a future supervisor—may re-assert your right to enforce the policy or procedure by going through what is known as a "due and proper notification process." This means that you must explain the policy or procedure to your staff. And, at the same time, you must tell them of your intention to enforce the rule in the future.

Thus, if there is a work rule, policy or procedure that, for some reason, has never been enforced in the past—and there is a desire to start enforcing it, you must tell your staff that it will be enforced. And, you must explain the work rule, policy or procedure to them.

You must go through this process before you make any attempt to enforce the policy or work rule.

List the two duties that you must perform during the "due and proper notification process."

- _____
- _____

(16)

Investigations

Disciplinary actions taken against an officer for violating a policy or breaking a rule can affect an officer's job and career. For example, if there is a serious violation, the employee may be suspended from work pending the outcome of the investigation. And if found guilty, the employee may be reprimanded, suspended or even discharged.

You must conduct a thorough and unbiased investigation, therefore, before you decide on a disciplinary action. This means that you must look into the employee's side of the story and collect any evidence or other information needed to arrive at a proper decision. By "checking out the employee's side," you may even uncover facts that indicate he or she did not violate policy or break a rule. It's better to find out that you don't have a case before you take any action and adversely affect an officer's career.

In addition to being thorough, you must convey to others that you are acting in an unbiased way. Be sure to avoid prejudicial remarks or comments that indicate presumption of guilt. This way, your staff will see that you are merely interested in getting the facts—not trying to "get the goods" on their co-worker.

TRUE/FALSE It's usually a waste of time to check out the employee's side of the story.
(10)

TRUE/FALSE The purpose of a disciplinary investigation is to make sure that guilty staff are fired.
(3)

Which of the following statements are NOT appropriate during a disciplinary investigation?

_____ A. "I see Hoover is under investigation. What did he do this time?"

_____ B. "Officer Heath is a good worker. I know he didn't do anything wrong."

_____ C. "I always thought Carpelli was up to something. Now we've got her!"

_____ D. "They never should have hired Sutts; I knew he'd screw up."

(19)

Evidence and Proof; Setting Penalties

In a discipline case, the burden of proof is on you and your agency. After all, you initiated the action. The standard of proof, however, is not as severe as a criminal case. Instead of proving "guilt beyond a reasonable doubt" (roughly 95% certainty of guilt), you need prove only a "preponderance of the evidence" (more than 50% certainty).

Generally, the amount of evidence required to sustain a disciplinary action increases with the severity of the penalty. Your word may be enough to sustain a written warning, but you would need more evidence to sustain a discharge. Such evidence might include statements from witnesses, and documentation in the form of reports or other written materials.

The charges you can bring for a violation of work rules are outlined in your agency's policy manual. This manual also lists the possible penalties for each offense.

For example, if the charge is "Failure or delay in carrying out orders, work assignments or instructions of superiors," the penalty range for a first offense might be "Official reprimand to removal." If the officer has been charged with this before, the penalty range is "15-day suspension to removal."

Later in this chapter, we will cover the things that you must consider in determining the charge and the penalty.

TRUE/FALSE The burden of proof in a discipline case is usually on the employee.

(4)

The Supervisor's Responsibility— Summary

In summary, policies and work rules are necessary to:

▶ Ensure that the agency meets its goals or mission,

▶ Have a standardized staff response to a given situation, and

▶ Protect the welfare of both staff and inmates.

As a supervisor, you are responsible for enforcing policies and work rules, and for taking action when violations occur. Enforcing the rules and policies fairly and consistently will help you maintain discipline in your unit.

The basis for evaluating how well you maintained discipline is whether you acted responsibly. The checklist below can help you determine where you stand in a particular situation.

Disciplinary Checklist	Yes	No
1. Clearly communicated policy or work rule	——	——
2. Consistently enforced policy or work rule	——	——
3. Conducted a thorough and unbiased investigation	——	——
4. Collected enough evidence to meet the standard of proof	——	——
5. Selected proper penalty	——	——

Discipline—
Case Study

BACKGROUND

You supervise the four employees below. Read each of the following summaries, and decide how you would handle each case.

MEL MULLIGAN

Information known to you:

Mulligan is the unit secretary. You noticed that the unit had been using a lot of ribbons for the computer printer and questioned Mulligan about the heavy use. Mulligan admitted to taking some of the ribbons home to use on her home computer printer. She has been a good employee, and you are surprised to find that she has been taking printer ribbons. She claims that everyone takes some "stuff" home, but they are not important items—things like pens and pencils, paper, ribbons and so forth. She feels that "it's part of her pay."

Rank in order, 1 to 5, the things you would do, with 1 being the first and 5 the last.

_____ A. Conduct an investigation of missing items.

_____ B. Interview the other staff to find out their attitude about taking minor items home.

_____ C. Check the policy about staff taking minor items home.

_____ D. Have a staff meeting to review the policy and explain how you will enforce it.

_____ E. Review the policy with Mel and tell her of your decision on the disciplinary action.

(26)

As Mel's supervisor, what would you recommend as the appropriate disciplinary action?

_____

_____

_____

_____

(31)

Discipline—
Case Study (continued)

TOM DONOVAN

Information known to you:

While returning home from an official training session in a county vehicle, Donovan ran off the road and damaged the front fender of the car. Police on the scene charged him with driving while intoxicated. You were not aware that Donovan had a drinking problem.

As his supervisor, what do you do?

_____
_____
_____
_____
_____
_____
_____
_____
_____
_____
_____
_____
_____
_____
_____

(17)

Discipline—
Case Study (continued)

HANK PATTERSON

Information known to you:

An inmate who had a female visitor claimed that Officer Patterson made lewd remarks to his girlfriend. There were no other witnesses. However, four months ago, Patterson was accused of asking another inmate's visitor for her phone number. He denied the accusation, but it was overheard by another correctional officer. You verbally reprimanded Patterson for that previous violation.

Evaluate each of the possible actions you might take and explain why you think the action is appropriate or not appropriate.

Talk to Patterson and tell him what the inmate said and that you'll be watching him closely to make sure that it's not true.

___ Appropriate   ___ Not appropriate

Because _____
_____
_____
_____
_____

(36)

Have Patterson and the inmate confront each other in your office, so you can see who is lying.

___ Appropriate   ___ Not appropriate

Because _____
_____
_____
_____
_____

(39)

Discipline—
Case Study (continued)

Because there are no witnesses, tell the inmate there is nothing you can do.

_____ Appropriate   _____ Not appropriate

Because _____
_____
_____
_____
_____

(23)

Meet with Patterson and tell him that you are going to investigate to determine if disciplinary action is warranted. Explain that you are doing this because of the previous case, and this inmate's complaint.

_____ Appropriate   _____ Not appropriate

Because _____
_____
_____
_____
_____

(27)

Discipline—
Case Study (continued)

ALICE PEACH

Information known to you:

You have had several reports indicating that Peach may be supplying inmates with cocaine. You confront her and request that she submit to a search, which is within the rules of your agency. She refuses to be searched.

As her supervisor, what do you do?

_____
_____
_____
_____
_____
_____
_____
_____
_____
_____
_____
_____
_____
_____

(21)

Pursuing Disciplinary Actions

This section of the chapter will concentrate on your role in pursuing disciplinary actions. We will deal with conducting investigations, determining charges and determining penalties.

Keep in mind as you read this section that many jurisdictions have approaches that vary from the one presented. The variety of procedures exists because of union contracts, state or county regulations and/or federal guidelines. The general principles presented here, however, apply to all situations. They will guide you through any disciplinary actions you must take.

In general, following agency rules about employee discipline is very important. In many cases, the supervisor's failure to properly follow the rules is grounds for dismissing the disciplinary action against the employee.

Conducting Investigations

The first thing that you should do when you suspect one of your employees has violated a policy or a work rule is to conduct a thorough and unbiased investigation of the incident. This practice conveys to others that you are alert and concerned about the behavior of your staff. And, perhaps even more important, it allows you to gather facts when they're fresh in people's minds.

Conducting the investigation promptly is especially important when an employee is suspended pending the findings of the investigation. If an employee is suspended and later found innocent of any contract or work rule violation he will, of course, be reimbursed for the time lost during his suspension.

The proper time to conduct an investigation is

_____

_____.

(24)

Conducting Investigations (continued)

When conducting an investigation, you should carefully take notes. Here it is useful to remember the five "W's" that reporters use in preparing their stories. Find out:

- *Who* was involved
- *When* the incident occurred
- *Where* the incident occurred
- *What* specifically happened
- *Why* the incident occurred

Be sure to write down all times, dates, places, persons interviewed and direct quotations from witnesses.

Sometimes, people involved in a disciplinary situation become upset or angry. Understanding what an agitated person is saying can be extremely difficult. It is important, therefore, to double check what you have written. To ensure accuracy, have the person review and approve the statements or quotations that you wrote down. This way, you'll know you "got it right."

Taking notes is important because of the length of time it often takes for a disciplinary action to come to a hearing. Over a period of time, your memory of what happened or what was said will fade. Your notes, however, will contain *all* of the information you collected during the investigation. There will be no gaps or missing information.

List the five basic facts that you should determine during an investigation.

- _____
- _____
- _____
- _____
- _____

(30)

Conducting Investigations (continued)

The cornerstone of an unbiased investigation is the demonstrated willingness on your part to collect all of the facts that are relevant in a given case. Once again, be sure to look into the employee's side of the story. If the employee says that there were witnesses who can support his or her story or that there are documents available which would do the same, you must investigate these claims.

Once you have collected all of the facts in the case, you should discuss them with your superior. If it appears that a violation *did* occur and that some disciplinary action will be necessary, both you and your superior should make a tentative decision about the proper charge.

The chart on the following page is from one agency's policy manual. It is just an example—check your agency's policy manual for the proper charges in your facility.

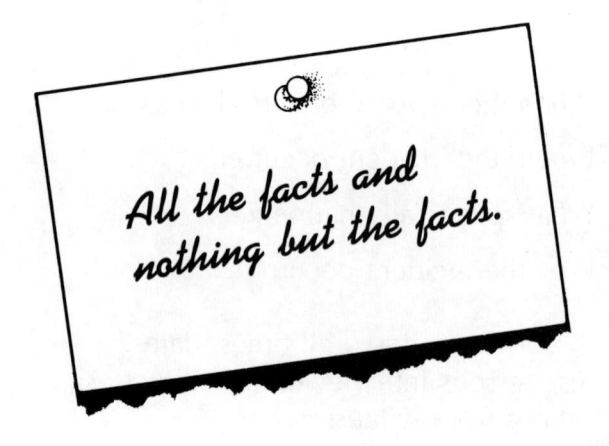

All the facts and nothing but the facts.

By looking into the employee's side of the story, you can sometimes determine _____ the violation occurred.

(28)

TRUE/FALSE   After you gather all the facts about a case, you should discuss them with the employee who violated the rules.

(35)

Sample List of Offenses and Disciplinary Actions

Nature of Offense	Explanation	First Offense	Second Offense	Third Offense	Reckoning Period
1. Unexcused or unauthorized absence of 8 hours or less.	Unauthorized absence of 8 hours of less, tardiness, leaving the job without permission.	Official reprimand to 1-day suspension	Official reprimand to 5-day suspension	Official reprimand to removal	6 mos.
2. Unexcused or unauthorized absence of between 1 and 5 consecutive workdays.	Unauthorized absence of 8 to 40 hours.	1-day to 5-day suspension	5-day suspension to 15-day suspension	15-day suspension to removal	1 yr.
3. Excessive unauthorized absence.	Unauthorized absence of more than 5 consecutive workdays.	5-day suspension to removal	15-day suspension to removal	Removal	2 yrs.
4. Careless workmanship or negligence resulting in spoilage or waste of materials or delay in work production.		Official reprimand to removal	15-day suspension to removal	Removal	2 yrs.
5. Failure or delay in carrying out orders, work assignments, or instructions of superiors.		Official reprimand to removal	15-day suspension to removal	Removal	2 yrs.
6. Failure to honor just debts without good cause.	A just financial obligation is one acknowledged by the employee, reduced to judgment by a court or imposed by law.	Official reprimand	Official reprimand	Reprimand to removal	2 yrs.
7. Loafing, wasting time, sleeping on the job, or inattention to duty.	Potential danger to safety of persons and/or actual damage to property is a consideration in determining severity of the penalty.	Official reprimand to removal	15-day suspension to removal	Removal	2 yrs.

Disciplinary Case Study— "The Incident"

BACKGROUND

At the Northeast State Prison, Officer Dick Brown reported to Sergeant Waters who was giving out the assignments for the shift. He told Brown to take Officer Hanns with him, pick up an inmate, and transport her to the forensic center for an examination.

Brown confronted Waters in front of the group and told him that it wasn't his turn for that kind of assignment. He always got stuck with the stuff someone else should do. After all, they'd be tied up all day and possibly overlap into the afternoon shift. During his outburst, Brown frequently used obscenities to get his point across. Waters told Brown that he had reviewed all the special assignments for the past two weeks—along with today's staffing needs—and wanted him to do it. Brown got up and left with Officer Hanns to transport the inmate.

Information known to you:

You are Sergeant Waters. You are a veteran supervisor at the Northeast State Prison, and you are known as a stickler for the rules. You try and rotate any special assignments but do not think that you should have to explain every decision you make. You know that Brown is a satisfactory performer but a perpetual complainer. To him, the department never does anything right.

Officer Brown has been told on previous occasions to improve his attitude toward supervisors, but this is the first time he has said something like this in front of others. No disciplinary action has ever been taken against him.

Disciplinary Case Study—
"The Incident" (continued)

Check each of the questions/statements you should include in your interview of Officer Dick Brown.

_____ A. Officer Brown, your behavior is very annoying.

_____ B. Officer Brown, I didn't appreciate your use of obscenities.

_____ C. Officer Brown, I called this hearing to discuss your outright refusal of a direct order and your use of obscenities.

_____ D. As I recall, you had no reason to let off steam.

_____ E. As I recall, I assigned you to take Officer Hanns with you, pick up an inmate and transport her to the Forensic Center. And you refused.

_____ F. You acted like a little kid.

_____ G. You know I don't owe anyone any explanations for my decisions.

_____ H. With your attitude, I don't know how you got as far as you did.

_____ I. I don't care what you have to say.

_____ J. Can you explain why you acted the way you did?

(29)

As the supervisor, what would you recommend as the proper disciplinary action?

_____ A. Verbal warning

_____ B. Written warning

_____ C. Suspension

(14)

Disciplinary Case Study— "I'm Sick Today"

BACKGROUND

Officer McIntyre is an average performer who has been with the Columbus County Sheriff's Department for three years. In the last six months, McIntyre has used his sick leave as fast as he got it. He has no major illness or injury. He usually calls in sick one day at a time on a weekend night or a night in conjunction with his days off. Sergeant Most has spoken to him twice and warned him about this apparent abuse of sick leave.

This week, McIntyre called in sick on a Saturday night when the department had two special functions to cover in addition to the normal patrol duties. He called from his cottage, three hours away, where he had been fishing all day.

Information known to you:

You are Sergeant Most. You have been a jail supervisor for the Columbus County Sheriff's Department for two years. Prior to that, you were a road patrol officer for three years and a corrections officer for three years.

You have just reviewed the weekend reports and noticed that Corrections Officer McIntyre called in sick on Saturday night. It is noted that the weekend supervisor tried to call his home, but there was no answer. You have spoken to Officer McIntyre twice before and warned him about his excessive use of sick leave.

Corrections Officer Hamway told you that, on Friday, McIntyre had been talking about going fishing for the weekend. Today, you overheard other officers making references to McIntyre being sick and laughing about it.

Disciplinary Case Study—
"I'm Sick Today" (continued)

Check each of the questions/statements you should include in your interview of Officer McIntyre.

_____ A. Officer McIntyre, how many reprimands have you already had about using sick leave?

_____ B. Officer McIntyre, you are a liar.

_____ C. Other officers tell me you like to fish.

_____ D. The reason I called you here is to discuss your frequent use of sick leave.

_____ E. Don't you think we'd all like a vacation?

_____ F. The way you're behaving, you'll never get promoted.

_____ G. I understand you called in sick on Saturday night. I also understand that no one answered the phone at your home when the supervisor called.

_____ H. Would you like to explain why you are absent so frequently?

_____ I. Were you fishing?

_____ J. Officer Hamway told me on Friday that you had been talking about going fishing for the weekend.

(44)

As the supervisor, what would you recommend as the proper disciplinary action?

_____ A. Verbal warning

_____ B. Written warning

_____ C. Suspension

(32)

CHAPTER 3: THE DISCIPLINARY PROCESS   III–163

Determining the Proper Charge

When a work rule or policy has been violated and you take disciplinary action against an employee, you need to determine the proper charge. In some cases, more than one charge can be brought for the same incident. For instance, a single incident may justify charges of poor work, insubordination, abusive language toward a supervisor and other charges.

However, it is usually a mistake to "throw the book at an employee" or take an action based on multiple charges. A better strategy is to select one charge that can be proven. Your proof comes from the statements and facts you gathered during the investigation, including the employee's side of the story. Then, at the hearing, state that other events occurred which could have warranted additional charges or actions—but you "set them aside" to be completely fair with the employee.

When you determine the proper charge, it is important to stick to a charge that _____ .

(38)

Determining the Proper Penalty

INTRODUCTION

When you're determining the penalty in a disciplinary case, you should consider a number of things. The first is whether the offense is a major, or a minor one.

Major offenses are those that are so serious that discharge is the only appropriate penalty regardless of any other circumstances or considerations. These actions are an immediate threat to the orderly administration of the institution and to the safety of the staff and inmates.

Minor offenses are, of course, less serious. While these actions are violations of the agency's policies, they are not an immediate threat to the operation of the institution or the well-being of staff and inmates.

Most of the offenses that you must deal with will be minor. When you set penalties for lesser offenses, you should follow the principle of corrective discipline. This principle says that the purpose of disciplinary procedures is to correct and save employees, not to punish them.

That is why correctional agencies frequently use a range of penalties. Most penalty sequences begin with verbal warnings, go on to written warnings and disciplinary layoffs, and end with discharge as a last resort.

The penalty sequence used in your agency may be different from that found in another one. However, most agencies use the principle of corrective discipline to establish a sequence of progressively more severe penalties. Consult your policies and procedures manual for the specific penalties suggested by your agency.

What is the principle of corrective discipline?

_____

_____

_____

(42)

TRUE/FALSE   The sequence of penalties in all corrections departments is verbal warning, written warning, discharge.

(45)

CHAPTER 3: THE DISCIPLINARY PROCESS   III–165

Determining the Proper Penalty (continued)

MINOR OFFENSES

To decide upon the correct penalty in the case of a lesser offense, you must always consider the following five factors.

▶ The seriousness of the offense

▶ The employee's disciplinary and work record

▶ The employee's length of service

▶ The organization's past practice in similar cases

▶ Mitigating or aggravating circumstances

The next part of the chapter will examine these factors in detail.

Determining the Proper Penalty (continued)

SERIOUSNESS OF THE OFFENSE

The first factor you must consider in determining the proper penalty is the *seriousness of the offense.*

Certainly, some offenses have a more immediate and adverse impact on the organization or its employees than others. Theft is an example of an offense that can vary a great deal in its seriousness. It is not very bad to steal a few pencils to give to one's children. It is much worse to steal quantities of food or beverages, however, from the institutional kitchen.

TRUE/FALSE All violations of a particular rule have the same degree of seriousness.

(34)

Determining the
Proper Penalty (continued)

EMPLOYEE'S RECORD

You should also consider the *employee's disciplinary and work records*. Does the employee have a clean disciplinary record? Was disciplinary action taken against him before? Is his job performance good? What rating did you give him on his last performance appraisal?

Looking at the work and discipline records should tell you if you are dealing with an incorrigible employee who is a threat, or a basically good employee who has strayed off the track. You can probably correct the behavior of the good employee with a verbal warning.

On the other hand, if the employee has had disciplinary actions before and shows poor job performance, you may be dealing with someone who is doing more harm than good on the job. You may need to give this employee a more severe penalty, such as a written warning.

Check the employee's past records!

TRUE/FALSE An employee's work record should not be a factor in determining the penalty in a disciplinary action.

(40)

Determining the Proper Penalty (continued)

EMPLOYEE'S RECORD (continued)

When you review an employee's prior disciplinary actions, you should remember the "reckoning period." The reckoning period is the amount of time that past offenses stay on an employee's personnel record.

For example, if Officer Barber received a written warning four or five years ago and has now violated another work rule, the prior warning should not be held against him. The long record of good service in those years indicates that Barber corrected his behavior.

Unless the contract at your agency specifies otherwise, the reckoning period for prior disciplinary actions is two years. This means that you can ignore written warnings that are more than two years old.

LENGTH OF SERVICE

When setting the penalty for a lesser offense, you should also consider the employee's *length of service*. A long record of good service to the department is a sign that a basically good employee has strayed. You should make every effort to correct your subordinate's behavior, rather than to severely discipline him or her.

When considering an employee's prior disciplinary actions, you should remember the _____ _____ for past offenses.
(33)

TRUE/FALSE   A long record of good service excuses an employee from disciplinary action for a lesser offense.
(41)

Determining the Proper Penalty (continued)

PAST PRACTICES

Another important factor in setting a penalty in a discipline case is the *organization's past practice* in similar or identical cases. If a work rule violation occurred before, and the circumstances are similar, you must use the same penalty. If you give different penalties for cases that are very similar, it is not only inconsistent, it looks like favoritism. As a good supervisor, you need to treat all your staff equally, with no signs of playing favorites.

Remember, however, that just because the same work rule violation has occurred does not mean that the circumstances are the same. Many supervisors see that the same work rule has been violated and give the same penalty—without considering the circumstances. In some instances, different circumstances may warrant different penalties.

For example, Officer Benz and Officer James are both charged with taking cases of sodas out of the storeroom. Officer Benz has been with your facility for 10 years, has been graded "Excellent" on his performance appraisal for the past 8 years, and has had no prior disciplinary action against him. You give Officer Benz a 5-day suspension.

Officer James has worked there 5 years. His job performance has been satisfactory, but you have noted on his performance appraisal that he doesn't seem to be paying full attention to his job. Four years ago, he was charged with hitting an inmate, and was given a written reprimand. Last year, he often was late for his shift, and you gave him a verbal warning. In the present case, you put a written warning in his personnel file and gave him a 15-day suspension.

A supervisor should impose the same penalty for similar offenses when _____
_____.
(43)

TRUE/FALSE Penalties always must be the same for violations of the same work rule.
(48)

CHAPTER 3: THE DISCIPLINARY PROCESS

Determining the Proper Penalty (continued)

MITIGATING AND AGGRAVATING CIRCUMSTANCES

Finally, in setting the penalties for lesser offenses, you must give proper consideration to any *mitigating or aggravating circumstances.*

Mitigating circumstances are ones that argue in favor of the employee—things that argue for a lesser penalty or perhaps no penalty at all. In the case of a fight, for instance, a mitigating circumstance could be that Smith did not throw the first punch, even though he may have been a little too aggressive in his defense.

Aggravating circumstances are just the opposite. These are things that make the violation worse than it might normally be. Aggravating circumstances argue for a more severe penalty. For instance, Jones not only refused to obey a direct order but also used abusive language toward her supervisor. The refusal to obey the order is a lesser offense. The use of abusive language, however, is an aggravating circumstance that makes the offense more serious.

Mitigating = in favor of the employee
Aggravating = against the employee

Define mitigating circumstances.

_____

_____

(9)

Define aggravating circumstances.

_____

_____

(47)

CHAPTER 3: THE DISCIPLINARY PROCESS   III—171

Determining the Proper Penalty (continued)

MAJOR OFFENSES

Major offenses are those that are so serious that discharge is the only appropriate penalty, regardless of any other circumstances or considerations.

There is no precise list of actions that are considered major offenses. However, these examples would normally fall into this category:

▶ Physical assault on a staff member

▶ Physical abuse of prisoners, visitors or others

▶ Sabotage of the equipment or mission

▶ Refusal to obey a proper order under emergency circumstances

Place a check next to the acts that would be considered major offenses.

_____ A. **Threatening another staff member**

_____ B. **Smuggling contraband into the facility**

_____ C. **Talking back to a supervisor**

_____ D. **Physically abusing inmates**

_____ E. **Stealing a spoon from the cafeteria**

(37)

Determining the
Proper Penalty—Summary

In summary, the only proper penalty in the case of major offenses is discharge. In the case of lesser offenses, however, you must always consider the seriousness of the offense, the employee's length of service and disciplinary record, the employee's work record, the organization's past practice in similar or identical cases, and any mitigating or aggravating circumstances before you set the penalty.

Otherwise, you may set a penalty that will not be upheld by higher levels of management.

Discipline Case Study

BACKGROUND

The staff of the intake unit at the Bellerumon Correctional Facility are routinely assigned to inmate transportation duties. These assignments include medical, court, or transfer to other facility groups.

Officer Washington usually leaves his transport partner alone with the inmate and goes off to conduct personal business. He has been warned about this twice. His attitude is that instead of just waiting at the hospital or court for hours on end, he will make constructive use of his time. Therefore, he feels justified in running personal errands, like picking up laundry or prescriptions. There has never been an incident where an inmate in Washington's charge has escaped or caused any other problems.

Information known to you:

You are Supervisor Grant. You have been a supervisor for ten years.

Washington has had two official warnings about his abuse of official time. He has been with the department for two years. You know that correctional work is not a career goal for Washington.

As the supervisor, what would you recommend as the proper disciplinary action?

_____ A. Verbal warning

_____ B. Written warning

_____ C. Suspension

_____ D. Dismissal

(46)

Summary

Let's summarize the main points in this chapter.

▶ Policies and work rules are necessary:
- To ensure that the agency meets its goals and mission
- To protect the welfare of both staff and inmates
- To ensure a standardized staff response to a given situation

▶ The enforcement of policies, procedures and work rules is necessary:
- To ensure the safety of staff and inmates
- To stop the negative behavior and maintain staff morale

▶ The six areas of supervisory responsibility in disciplining staff are:
- Communicating the rules and policies
- Enforcing the rules consistently
- Conducting investigations properly
- Gathering evidence and proof
- Determining the proper charge
- Setting penalties

▶ Major offenses are those offenses that are considered to be so serious that discharge is the only appropriate penalty regardless of any other circumstances or considerations. These actions are an immediate threat to the orderly administration of the institution and to the safety of the staff and inmates.

▶ Minor offenses are those which, while violations of policy, are not an immediate threat to the operation of the institution or the well-being of staff and inmates. Minor offenses are resolved through warnings, reprimands and suspensions.

▶ The five factors that supervisors must consider when setting the penalty for a minor offense are:
- The seriousness of the offense
- The employee's disciplinary and work record
- The employee's length of service
- The agency's past practice in similar cases
- Mitigating or aggravating circumstances

Answer Key— The Disciplinary Process

1. One way to maintain discipline is by **enforcing the work rules.**

2. Failing to consistently enforce a policy or work rule may establish a **past precedent.**

3. **False.** The purpose of the investigation is to *get the facts*.

4. **False.** The burden of proof is on the supervisor and the agency. In other words, you need to prove your case against the employee with more than 50% certainty.

5. The continued violation of rules could eventually jeopardize the **safety** of staff and inmates.

6. **False.** It is the non-enforcement of policies and procedures over a long period of time that establishes a precedent.

7. **True.** Some of your staff will break work rules but probably only a small percentage of your unit will do so.

8. **True.**

9. Mitigating circumstances argue in favor of the employee and may be the basis for a lesser penalty, or no penalty at all.

10. **False.** If you are involved in conducting a disciplinary investigation, you must be thorough and unbiased in your approach, and gather all the facts from every possible source, including the charged employee.

11. **False.** Why should the employee stop if he or she is not disciplined for the violations?

12. **False.** Disciplinary procedures should be a last resort, used only after you have tried performance evaluation, coaching and training.

13. **Yes.** Past precedent applies because the act of depositing inmate mail was done over a long period of time with the supervisor's knowledge and approval (he didn't try to stop it).

Answer Key—
The Disciplinary Process (continued)

14. The proper disciplinary action would be:

    ____ A. Verbal warning

    ____ B. Written warning

    √ C. Suspension

15. **True.**

16. The two duties that you must perform during the "due and proper notification process" are:

    - Tell your staff what the policy or procedure is
    - Tell your staff that you are going to enforce the policy

17. As Donovan's supervisor, you should:

    - Review the police report to verify the facts
    - Talk to Donovan to see if there were unusual circumstances
    - Recommend that Donovan report to your agency's personnel counselor

18. **False.** Only a very small percentage of your staff will be involved in any form of disciplinary action.

19. The following statements are NOT appropriate during a disciplinary investigation:

    √ A. "I see Hoover is under investigation. What did he do this time?"

    √ B. "Officer Heath is a good worker. I know he didn't do anything wrong."

    √ C. "I always thought Carpelli was up to something. Now we've got her!"

    √ D. "They never should have hired Sutts; I knew he'd screw up."

20. **True.**

21. As Peach's supervisor, you should:

    - Review the policy on staff searches, or consult your superior
    - Talk to Peach; explain the policy on staff searches and the consequences of her not following the policy

Answer Key—
The Disciplinary Process (continued)

22. The reasons why work rules and policies are necessary include:
    - To ensure that the agency meets it goals or mission
    - To protect the welfare of both staff and inmates
    - To have a standardized staff response to a given situation

23. **Not appropriate.** You cannot assume that there is nothing you can do. Get all the facts of the case.

24. The proper time to conduct an investigation is **as soon as possible after the suspected violation has occurred.**

25. The ways to communicate policies and work rules to employees include:
    - Have a one-on-one discussion, especially with a new employee
    - Have a one-on-one or small group discussion, especially when there is a change in policy or procedure
    - Post a notice on the staff bulletin board
    - Distribute an employee handbook and/or a policies and procedures manual

26. There may be no "right" answer on a sequence of actions on your part, but a good choice would be:

    | 3 | A. | Conduct an investigation of missing items. |
    | 4 | B. | Interview the other staff to find out their attitude about taking minor items home. |
    | 1 | C. | Check the policy about staff taking minor items home. |
    | 5 | D. | Have a staff meeting to review the policy and explain how you will enforce it. |
    | 2 | E. | Review the policy with Mel and tell her of your decision on the disciplinary action. |

Answer Key—
The Disciplinary Process (continued)

27. **Appropriate.** There is enough reason to investigate. However, as a supervisor, you must be unbiased in regard to Patterson. Maybe the inmate is trying to get back at Patterson, or maybe Patterson is guilty. The only way to find out is to conduct an investigation.

28. By looking into the employee's side of the story, you can sometimes determine **why (or even if)** the violation occurred.

29. The questions/statements you should include in your interview of Officer Dick Brown are:

    _____ A. Officer Brown, your behavior is very annoying.

    _____ B. Officer Brown, I didn't appreciate your use of obscenities.

    √ C. Officer Brown, I called this hearing to discuss your outright refusal of a direct order and your use of obscenities.

    _____ D. As I recall, you had no reason to let off steam.

    √ E. As I recall, I assigned you to take Officer Hanns with you, pick up an inmate and transport her to the Forensic Center. And you refused.

    _____ F. You acted like a little kid.

    _____ G. You know I don't owe anyone any explanations for my decisions.

    _____ H. With your attitude, I don't know how you got as far as you did.

    _____ I. I don't care what you have to say.

    √ J. Can you explain why you acted the way you did?

30. The five basic facts that you should determine during an investigation are:

    - Who was involved
    - When the incident occurred
    - Where the incident occurred
    - What specifically happened
    - Why the incident occurred

Answer Key—
The Disciplinary Process (continued)

31. The appropriate disciplinary action would be a verbal reprimand with a caution that any further theft on her part would lead to an *official* disciplinary action. This response is sufficient because she is a good employee, and the items taken were minor.

32. The proper disciplinary action would be:
    - _____ A. Verbal warning
    - __✓__ B. Written warning
    - _____ C. Suspension

33. When considering an employee's prior disciplinary actions, you should remember the **reckoning period** for past offenses.

34. **False.** Violations of a particular rule *vary* in their degree of seriousness.

35. **False.** Once you have completed the investigation, you should discuss your findings with your *superior*.

36. **Not appropriate.** You either take action, or you don't; you should never threaten.

37. The acts that would be considered major offenses are:
    - _____ A. Threatening another staff member
    - __✓__ B. Smuggling contraband into the facility
    - _____ C. Talking back to a supervisor
    - __✓__ D. Physically abusing inmates
    - _____ E. Stealing a spoon from the cafeteria

38. When you determine the proper charge, it is important to stick to a charge that **can be proven.**

39. **Not appropriate.** Both men will simply restate their cases. Also, it is very poor supervision on your part because you will not get information when they are both there. You should question them independently and use this as the basis of an investigation.

Answer Key—
The Disciplinary Process (continued)

40. **False.** An employee's work record *should* be considered in determining the penalty in a disciplinary action.

41. **False.** A long record of good service argues strongly on the employee's behalf, but it does not excuse him or her from disciplinary action.

42. The principle of corrective discipline is that **the purpose of disciplinary procedures is to correct and save employees, not to punish them.**

43. A supervisor should impose the same penalty for similar offenses when **the circumstances are very similar.**

44. The questions/statements you should include in your interview of Officer McIntyre are:

    - ✓ A. Officer McIntyre, how many reprimands have you already had about using sick leave?
    - ___ B. Officer McIntyre, you are a liar.
    - ___ C. Other officers tell me you like to fish.
    - ✓ D. The reason I called you here is to discuss your frequent use of sick leave.
    - ___ E. Don't you think we'd all like a vacation?
    - ___ F. The way you're behaving, you'll never get promoted.
    - ✓ G. I understand you called in sick on Saturday night. I also understand that no one answered the phone at your home when the supervisor called.
    - ✓ H. Would you like to explain why you are absent so frequently?
    - ___ I. Were you fishing?
    - ✓ J. Officer Hamway told me on Friday that you had been talking about going fishing for the weekend.

45. **False.** Corrections departments may vary in their sequence of penalties.

Answer Key—
The Disciplinary Process (continued)

46. As the supervisor, the proper disciplinary action you would recommend should be:

    _____ A. Verbal warning

    _____ B. Written warning

    __✓__ C. Suspension

    _____ D. Dismissal

47. Aggravating circumstances argue against the employee and may be the basis for a more severe penalty.

48. **False.** Penalties can vary for violations of the same work rule, depending upon all the circumstances of the case.

References

Allen, Harry E., and Clifford E. Simonsen. *Corrections in America: An Introduction.* 5th ed. New York: MacMillan Publishing Co., 6th ed., 1992.

American Correctional Association. *Correctional Officer Resource Guide.* Laurel, MD: American Correctional Association, 1989.

American Correctional Association. *Correctional Officers: Power, Pressure, and Responsibility.* Laurel, MD: American Correctional Association, 1983.

American Correctional Association. *Legal Issues for Correctional Officers Correspondence Course.* Laurel, MD: American Correctional Association, 1989.

American Correctional Association. *Legal Issues for Probation and Parole Officers Correspondence Course.* Laurel, MD: American Correctional Association, 1988.

Anderson, Debra J. *Curbing the Abuses of Inmate Litigation.* College Park, MD: American Correctional Association, 1986.

Barrineau, H. E., III. *Civil Liability in Criminal Justice.* Cincinnati, OH: Anderson Publishing Company, 1987.

Bennis, Warren, and Burt Nanus. *Leaders: The Strategies for Taking Charge.* New York: Harper & Row, 1985.

Black's Law Dictionary 822, 6th ed., 1991.

Cheek, Frances E., and Marie DiStefano Miller. *Stress Management for Correctional Officers and Their Families.* Laurel, MD: American Correctional Association, 1984.

Collins, William C. *Correctional Law for the Correctional Officer.* Laurel, MD: American Correctional Association, 1993.

Craig, R. L. *Training and Development Handbook.* 3rd. ed. New York: McGraw Hill, 1987.

Del Carmen, Rolando V. "Legal Liabilities and Responsibilities of Corrections Agency Supervisors." *Federal Probation,* 1983.

Edwards, David V. *The American Political Experience.* Englewood Cliffs, NJ: Prentice-Hall, Inc., 1982.

Fisher, Margaret, Edward O'Brian, and David T. Austern. *Practical Law for Jail and Prison Personnel.* St. Paul, MN: West Publishing Company, 1987.

Fowler, Catherine. "The Supervisor as Trainer." National Institute of Corrections, 1983.

Glassman, Edward. "Creative Problem Solving: Habits That Need Changing." *Supervisory Management,* February 1989.

Gruber, Frank, ed. *The Manager's Guide to Better Supervision.* New York: The Research Institute of America, 1986.

Hersey, Paul. *The Situational Leader.* New York: Warner Books, 1984.

Hopkins-Doerr, Mike. "Getting More Out of MBWA." *Supervisory Management,* February 1989.

International City Management Association. *Effective Supervisory Practices.* Washington, DC: International City Management Association, 1986.

International Training, Research and Evaluation Council, for the National Institute of Corrections. *First- and Second-Line Jail Supervisors Instructor's Manual.* Boulder, CO: National Institute of Corrections, 1980.

Maccoby, Michael. *The Leader: A New Face for American Management.* New York: Ballantine Books, 1981.

Maryland Department of Corrections. "Management Seminar: The Troubled Employee," 1982.

National Institute for Citizen Education in the Law, for the National Institute of Corrections. *Legal Issues in Corrections, Instructor's Guide.* Boulder, CO: National Institute of Corrections, 1987.

National Sheriffs' Association. *Inmates' Legal Rights.* Alexandria, VA: National Sheriffs' Association, 1987.

Palmer, John W. *Constitutional Rights of Prisoners.* 4th ed. Cincinnati, OH: Anderson Publishing Company, 1991.

Petrocelli, William, and Barbara Kate Repa. *Sexual Harassment on the Job.* Berkeley, CA: Nolo Press, 1992.

Robinson, Cyril D. *Legal Rights, Duties and Liabilities of Criminal Justice Personnel, History and Analysis.* Springfield, IL: Charles C. Thomas, Publisher, 1984.

Rovner, Julie. "Americans with Disabilities Act." *Congressional Quarterly.* Washington, DC, 1990.

Sherman, A., G. Bohlander, and H. Chruden. *Managing Human Resources.* 8th ed. Cincinnati, OH: South Western Publishing Co., 1988.

Snarr, Richard W., and Bruce I. Wolford. *Introduction to Corrections.* Dubuque, IA: Wm. C. Brown Company Publishers, 1985.

St. John, Walter D. "Plain Speaking." *Personnel Journal,* June 1985.

The State of Corrections: Proceedings, ACA Annual Conferences, 1988. Laurel, MD: American Correctional Association, 1988.

University Research Corporation, for the National Institute of Corrections. *Legal Issues for Community Corrections Personnel, Trainer and Participant Guides.* Boulder, CO: National Institute of Corrections, 1988.

Vom Saal, Walter, and Wayne L. Trotta. "Managing the 3 Ps of Meetings." *Supervisory Management,* February 1989.

Zemke, Ron. "Should Supervisors Be Counselors?" *Training,* March 1983.